D1343595

Penny Red

Notes from the
New Age of Dissent

Laurie Penny

Foreword by
Warren Ellis

PlutoPress
www.plutobooks.com

First published 2011 by Pluto Press
345 Archway Road, London N6 5AA

www.plutobooks.com

Distributed in the United States of America exclusively by
Palgrave Macmillan, a division of St. Martin's Press LLC,
175 Fifth Avenue, New York, NY 10010

British Library Cataloguing in Publication Data
A catalogue record for this book is available from the British Library

ISBN   978 0 7453 3208 6 Paperback
ISBN   978 1 84964 605 5 Kindle eBook
ISBN   978 1 84964 603 1 eBook PDF
ISBN   978 1 84964 604 8 ePub

Library of Congress Cataloging in Publication Data applied for

This book is printed on paper suitable for recycling and made from
fully managed and sustained forest sources. Logging, pulping and
manufacturing processes are expected to conform to the
environmental standards of the country of origin.

10   9   8   7   6   5   4   3   2   1

Designed and produced for Pluto Press by Chase Publishing Services Ltd
Typeset from disk by Stanford DTP Services, Northampton, England
Simultaneously printed digitally by CPI Antony Rowe, Chippenham, UK and
Edwards Bros in the United States of America

Contents

Acknowledgements

Thanks to everyone at the *New Statesman* magazine for having faith in this body of work giving me a platform to write. Most of the articles that follow were published in the *New Statesman*, either online or in the reactionary hard-copy remix that a few subscribers seem to favour. Thanks are also due to David, Alec and everyone at Pluto Press; to the enchanting and inhumanly patient Juliet Pickering at A P Watt; to my friends and mentors, Paul Mason, Warren Ellis, China Miéville, Roz Kaveney, Tanya Gold, David Randall, Cath Howdle, Adrian Bott, Zoe Stavri and Jed Weightman.

Most of all, though, thanks and respect are due to the activists, anarchists, feminists, students, school pupils and pissed-off citizens around the world who have been part of what I've called 'the new age of dissent'. I have been privileged to meet some of them, and many more have contacted me, encouraging me to keep writing. Those letters and emails have made all the difference. As I write, many young activists and student protesters are serving lengthy jail sentences in Britain for taking part in peaceful demonstrations and for defending themselves against police violence. It is an outrage that they should have to be so brave. This book is dedicated to them, in solidarity, and to my father.

Foreword

Warren Ellis

One of the worst things in the world, for me, is switching on Twitter and seeing that Laurie Penny is loose on the streets of London. Because it inevitably means that there's some kind of protest action going on, and, equally inevitably, that Laurie's out in the middle of it. An element of the inward wince I experience is certainly down to the immediate and quite vivid recollection of having to put people back together after the Poll Tax riots in the 1990s. A bigger element is that, frankly, Laurie has all the self-preservation instinct of a lemming dipped in vodka and balanced on top of a stepladder. And so I worry. It's not, I hope, some paternal chauvinism. It's more that, having somehow survived to the age of 43, I remember both feeling immortal at 24 *and* how many people I've buried since then.

And it's not like times have changed. Sure, the SPG (Special Patrol Group) aren't operating any more. But now it turns out the Met are okay with beating the wheelchair-bound and killing passers-by live on video. And I'm damned sure the stark idiocy of kettling is going to get a copper killed one day soon, and that makes me sad and angry too. So, yeah, when I see her running around out there, it drives me a little nuts. I mean, I know she needs to do it. And I have a little guilt because one of her formative influences was a book I wrote, so when she does finally get the piss beaten out of her it's going to be a little bit my fault.

But this is what Laurie does. She drives you a little bit nuts. She makes you angry. Sometimes it's about something you're angry about too, and she shares it with you, and finds new ways to see it with you. Sometimes she makes you angry in that way that makes you want to hold her head down the toilet until her leg stops twitching. There are things in this collection that, honestly, give me a sudden compulsion to press a nerve in Laurie's neck, and I've been her friend for years. Everybody will find something in this book to argue with. And that's good. Laurie Penny makes you shout, but she also makes you think. Laurie Penny makes you *engage*, which is vital in a society that in the last 20 years had wandered a fair way towards turning passive acceptance into an artform.

Someone once said that if you want objective journalism, get yourself a CCTV camera. Subjective journalism isn't a crime. It's a joy and a necessity. Reportage needs to be a living thing. And I love Laurie, and I love this book, because it illustrates that, *yes,* there *is* going to be a new generation of reporters capable of getting up on their hind legs and shouting when things go wrong.

This book is, I think, as vivid and electric a snapshot of this moment as you'll find. I hope you enjoy it – and shout at it, and with it – as much as I did.

Warren Ellis
Southend-on-Sea
June 2011

Warren Ellis is the author of the graphic novels Transmetropolitan, Fell *and* Red *(amongst 50 others), and of the novel* Crooked Little Vein. *He is the recipient of the NUIG Lit & Deb Society's President's Medal for his contributions to freedom of speech.*

Introduction

'When the going gets weird, the weird turn pro.'
Hunter S. Thompson

'The truth may be out there, but the lies are inside your head.'
Terry Pratchett, *The Hogfather*

Politics, like alcohol, makes me feel horrible and sexy. So, with a ready deadline and in the absence of gin, let me share a moment with you.

Roaring down the Holloway Road one night not so long ago, hanging from the shoulders of a bemuscled friend and hollering misplaced intentions into the traffic, in what addicts call a moment of clarity, I realised how much we have left to do.

This generation has inherited, whether or not it deserves it, a world whose old order is broken, and parents who have no idea how to build a new one. We were raised to believe that if we worked hard and passed all the exams, everything would be all right. We were lied to. Everything is most certainly bloody not all right. However many times we're informed that we've been given the whole world on a cocktail stick, it is terribly hard to shake the creeping feeling that we're being worked over, every day, by idiots. This is because we are being worked over, every day, by idiots.

We are worked over by our gender, by our sexuality, by our class, our age, our race and nationality, by our money or lack of money, by the fact that we're young and poor and stupid, by whatever metal or plastic gods we've chosen to chase. If you've ever felt like control of your life is slipping through the cracks in your fists, this means you. If you've wanted something you could not name, this means you. This means us. Old and young, we are being worked over every day.

We do not have to take this.

This is a story about the new young left, dispersed and disenfranchised though we may be, and the resources we have available to us. It's about politics, feminism, alternative culture. Politics because without it we are armourless, powerless children. Feminism because it breaks in wherever the lines have been drawn between the weak and the strong. And alternative culture because we need to destroy their hallucinations with our desires. Because – just sometimes – if we want to win, we have to become the people our parents always warned us about.

Fortunately, this is eminently doable.

*   *   *

Four years have passed since I wrote those words as part of the first post on Penny Red, the blog which turned into the column which turned into this book. Back then the new young left had not yet properly emerged, no matter how hard some of us were wishing them into being. Then the bottom dropped out of the global economy, there were changes of government in Britain and America, and from Tahrir Square to the gates of Westminster people began really to ask, and not quietly, if another world might be possible. The people who were born after Francis Fukuyama declared the end of history are beginning to articulate to a paranoid global plutocracy that history is far from over, that freeing the markets has not freed the people, that there is a place in this bankrupt world for values and ideals. We are spinning in the amniotic fluid of history, nourished by new unorthodoxies. What follows is an attempt to record some of those unorthodoxies as they have arisen.

So that's that, and this is me. I'm Laurie, and I'm no-one special, apart from having a nagging problem with authority which has got me into trouble for as long as I can remember. At the age of ten, chance and parental whim enrolled me briefly in an evangelist Christian school, where I had my first stand-up fight with an adult in a position of power. When the teacher of religious indoctrination took us through the section of Genesis which instructs women to defer to their husbands on all matters, I suggested in no uncertain terms that this was dangerous bullshit. 'Be honest,' the teacher demanded. 'If it came to a tough decision in your life, wouldn't it make you feel safer to know there was a powerful man who would take control for you?'

The detention I subsequently received for ungodly language smarted far less than watching my classmates nod along with the teacher. I'm 24 years old now, which means I still know almost nothing about anything, but I know enough to question any smiling bastard who offers you a quiet life in exchange for good behaviour.

Most of the pieces collected here were written late at night, perched in filthy kitchens or expropriated buildings or on someone else's sofa, balancing the laptop on my knees and trying to block out the sounds of strung-out young people fighting and fucking. This is less a testament to wild bohemian affectations than to the fact that for the most of my early twenties, along with nearly all of my friends, I had no secure place to live. For the most part, I crammed my life into a small red suitcase, flinging myself frantically towards the slender hope of a safer future. There is no room for us anymore, for freaks and reprobates and ordinary young people who just want the chance to hold down a job in a world that isn't entirely on fire.

This is a precarious, paranoid culture, even in the spoilt heart of western capitalism that raised me. From 2007 to 2010, I bunkered down in a series of grimy, rat-infested communes in inner London, over two years of economic catastrophe, graduate debt and personal disaster, during which my closest friends and I watched our futures being progressively mortgaged by a political class which has betrayed its poorest constituents and broken the hearts of its children. We slept three to a room and lived on frozen pizza, toxic love-affairs and videogames ripped off the internet. Everyone got sick, everyone slid into anxiety and depression, and I spent several mornings sitting on my best friend's chest to stop him flinging himself from the second-storey window rather than face another trip to the Job Centre. There was no room for us in this brave new post-recession political settlement. There was quite literally no room.

At some point during the cruel, clammy summer of 2008, we realised that we had been lied to all our lives. We were told that if we worked very hard, passed all the exams, did as we were told and tried to look pretty, then health, happiness and a downpayment on a small flat in Surbiton would surely be ours. We were lied to, and now we had to try to build lives in the wreckage of those untruths. It was bad enough slurping down the dregs of the New Labour years, but by the time the Tories got in and started squatting with intent over what was left of welfare, healthcare and education, it was already far too late for far too many of us.

Not for me, of course. The reason I'm writing an introduction to a book of columns whilst many of my friends are in jail, destroying their sanity in call-centres or languishing on the dole is not talent, nor personal worth, but the simple fact that I got lucky. Even though it worked out in my favour, it would be a monstrous act of complicity not to open this book by acknowledging that I got lucky enough to get to where I am today inside a system that tantalises us with promises of personal transcendence before snapping closed those windows of opportunity.

I got lucky because I had a privileged education. I got lucky because I lived a life which let me get incredibly angry in relative safety. And I got lucky because I received, at the right moment, a small inheritance from a dead relative. That money pushed open – just a sliver but enough – those windows of privilege, cemented in unpaid internships and work experience, that slam shut on most young people trying to make their way in politics, finance, journalism, law, fashion or the arts in this city and every other city in the west.

So I got lucky and wriggled through the windows. But today they are shutting tighter all the time. And there comes a time when it all gets too much. There comes a time when you have to take your hands off the sill, make a fist and smash the glass.

When the first window was smashed at the headquarters of the party in government on 10 November 2010, I happened to be in the right place at the right time, with a phone that could do the internet. I started tweeting about what I saw, and later wrote a series of reports from the front lines of the London riots over that Christmas, reports that went viral around the world. Those articles are included in this collection in the chapter 'This is Actually Happening'. They are a flawed and incomplete attempt to tell a story that nobody else in the mainstream press was at that point telling, a story about a lost generation turning the whole world upside down in order to find itself. Many are already calling it 'the new 1968'. I am far from the only young activist who finds that aphorism decidedly unambitious. For one thing, it reduces the profound political reawakening taking place in Britain and elsewhere to a trajectory of inevitable failure. Anyone who has met, or indeed been, a young person in the developed world in the early twenty-first century, can assure you that the naysayers haven't quite grasped our ruthlessness, nor how little we have to lose.

Things are kicking off everywhere. Angry, dispossessed young people in Britain, America, Europe and the Middle East have shucked off the narrative of corporate serfdom, using the very technology that was supposed to make us atomised and apathetic to share ideas, build networks and organise horizontally. As I write, the backlash is on. Hundreds of activists have been beaten, arrested and are facing imprisonment in London. The flourishing of radical ideas has been met by a violent spasm of right-wing propaganda across the world, in countries where 'socialism' is a dirty word, where 'anarchism' means only hooligans in black smashing up shops, where 'feminism' is a synonym for dungaree-wearing, eyeball-rolling, murderous lesbianism and 'democracy' means wars of conquest across the Gulf. Now, more than ever, it's important for those of us who are brave and bright enough to question that reactionary kickback to maintain our voices, to remember that our ideas are valid, to go in everywhere, question everything. I hope that this book will add to the pile of tangible evidence that their consensus is not absolute, that there are those of us who think differently.

After the protest chronicle, there follow collections of articles about parliamentary politics, extra-parliamentary politics, reviews and interviews, and feminism. The 'Girl Trouble' chapter, in particular, branches out into every other aspect of the journalism collected here, because feminism is the cornerstone of my politics – it always has been, and always will be. I have always craved a radical context for feminism, a space where women's rights do not have to be a bourgeois ghetto. It seemed to me from the start of my work as a rookie journalist that, whilst feminist ideas were enjoying a small renaissance amongst educated young women in the west, that renaissance risked becoming an echo-chamber in which the 'enlightened' spoke only to one another.

More than anything, I wanted to speak about feminism in the same breath as anti-capitalism, as socialism, as radicalism and practical resistance. I wanted to make it clear that one cannot properly question patriarchy without questioning profit – and vice versa. I wanted to be part of a conversation where feminism was a fundamental part of the big political picture.

That conversation has not yet properly begun. Radicals and armchair revolutionaries across the world still fall eerily silent when the women in their midst begin to speak about their own struggles. Nothing brought that silence home more tragically than the reports that poured in over internet backchannels on 8 March 2011, the centenary of International Women's Day. On that day, female Egyptian protesters were beaten and sexually assaulted in Tahrir Square by the same men who, just weeks before, had stood side to side with them to topple Hosni Mubarak's 30-year regime.

Too many women continue to believe that their own problems, however urgent, are of no importance to the 'wider' world of power and politics. Too many men are happy for them to go on believing this to be the case, which is why political and cultural issues of immediate concern to over half the population of the planet are routinely relegated to the 'women's pages' in national newspapers.

No honest counter-culture can hope to succeed if it marginalises its women. If we want to win, we need to understand feminism as part of the answer to a system that cauterises human solidarity, destroys human pleasure, and replaces them with a violent, homogenous, artificial sexuality that can never be slaked. As a fumbling initiate in the world of political writing, I have tried, in my own way, to pull down the trousers of that sexuality. I have tried to anatomise the instruments of shame, violence and indoctrination that skewer the soft, weird core of our culture. I have tried, and inevitably I've made mistakes. I have been writing in a terrible hurry, because it feels like there's so little time.

Whenever anyone asks me what I hope for, I say what a lot of young people these days tend to say: I hope we have more time. It can often feel like time is running out, like history is closing down on us, like we're running to keep up, like in between school and work and death there's no time for error, or risk, or debate. We need to find the time for all of these things. I hope we do. I hope we find time to be brave. I hope we find time to build the future. I hope we find time to be kinder to one another. I hope, I hope, I hope. I hope many things, and right now I hope you enjoy this book.

London, June 2011

I
This is Actually Happening

'Hope is the thing with feathers, that perches in the soul
And sings the tune without the words, and never stops – at all.'
Emily Dickinson

INSIDE THE MILLBANK TOWER RIOTS

11 November 2010

It's a bright, cold November afternoon, and inside 30 Millbank, the headquarters of the Conservative Party, a line of riot police with shields and truncheons are facing down a groaning crowd of young people with sticks and smoke bombs.

Screams and the smash of trodden glass cram the foyer as the ceiling-high windows, entirely broken through, fill with some of the 52,000 angry students and schoolchildren who have marched through the heart of London today to voice their dissent to the government's savage attack on public education and public services. Ministers are cowering on the third floor, and through the smoke and shouting a young man in a college hoodie crouches on top of the rubble that was once the front desk of the building, his red hair tumbling into his flushed, frightened face.

He meets my eyes, just for a second. The boy, clearly not a seasoned anarchist, has allowed rage and the crowd to carry him through the boundaries of what was once considered good behaviour, and found no one there to stop him. The grown-ups didn't stop him. The police didn't stop him. Even the walls didn't stop him. His twisted expression is one I recognise in my own face, reflected in the screen as I type. It's the terrified exhilaration of a generation that's finally waking up to its own frantic power.

Glass is being thrown; I fling myself behind a barrier and scramble on to a ledge for safety. A nonplussed school pupil from south London has had the same idea. He grins, gives me a hand up and offers me a cigarette of which he is at least two years too young to be in possession. I find that my teeth are chattering and not just from cold. 'It's scary, isn't it?' I ask. The boy shrugs. 'Yeah,' he says, 'I suppose it is scary. But frankly...' He lights up, cradling the contraband fag, 'frankly, it's not half as scary as what's happening to our future'.

There are three things to note about this riot, the first of its kind in Britain for decades, that aren't being covered by the press. The first is that not all of the young people who have come to London to protest are university students. Lots are school pupils, and many of the 15-, 16- and 17-year-olds present have been threatened with expulsion or withdrawal of their EMA (education maintenance allowance) benefits if they chose to protest today. They are here anyway, alongside teachers, young working people and unemployed graduates.

What unites them? A chant strikes up: 'We're young! We're poor! We won't pay any more!'

The second is that this is not, as the right-wing news would have you believe, just a bunch of selfish college kids not wanting to pay their fees (many of the students here will not even be directly affected by the fee changes). This is about far more than university fees, far more even than the coming massacre of public education.

This is about a political settlement that has broken its promises not once but repeatedly, and proven that it exists to represent the best interests of the business community, rather than to be accountable to the people. The students I speak to are not just angry about fees, although the Liberal Democrats' U-turn on that issue is manifestly an occasion of indignation: quite simply, they feel betrayed. They feel that their futures have been sold in order to pay for the financial failings of the rich, and they are correct in their suspicions. One tiny girl in animal-print leggings carries a sign that reads: 'I've always wanted to be a bin man.'

The third and most salient point is that the violence kicking off around Tory HQ – and make no mistake, there is violence, most of it directed at government property – is not down to a 'small group of anarchists ruining it for the rest'. Not only are Her Majesty's finest clearly giving as good as they're getting, the vandalism is being committed largely by consensus – those at the front are being carried through by a groundswell of movement from the crowd.

Not all of those smashing through the foyer are in any way kitted out like your standard anarchist black-mask gang. These are kids making it up as they go along. A shy looking girl in a nice tweed coat and bobble hat ducks out of the way of some flying glass, squeaks in fright, but sets her lips determinedly and walks forward, not back, towards the line of riot cops. I see her pull up the neck of her pink polo-neck to hide her face, aping those who have improvised bandanas. She gives the glass under her feet a tentative stomp, and then a firmer one. Crunch, it goes. Crunch.

As more riot vans roll up and the military police move in, let's whisk back three hours and 300 metres up the road, to Parliament Square. The cold winter sun beats down on 52,000 young people pouring down Whitehall to the Commons. There are twice as many people here as anyone anticipated, and the barriers erected by the stewards can't contain them all: the demonstration shivers between the thump of techno sound systems and the stamp of samba drums, is a living, panting beast, taking a full hour to slough past Big Ben in all its honking glory. A brass band plays 'The Liberty Bell' while excited students yammer and dance and snap pictures on their phones. 'It's a party out here!' one excited posh girl tells her mobile, tottering on Vivienne Westwood boots, while a bunch of Manchester anarchists run past with a banner saying 'Fuck Capitalism'.

One can often take the temperature of a demonstration by the tone of the chanting. The cry that goes up most often at this protest is a thunderous, wordless roar, starting from the back of the crowd and reverberating up and down Whitehall. There are no words. It's a shout of sorrow and celebration and solidarity and it slices through the chill winter air like a knife to the stomach of a trauma patient. Somehow, the pressure has been released and the rage of Europe's young people is flowing free after a year, two years, ten years of poisonous capitulation.

They spent their childhoods working hard and doing what they were told with the promise that one day, far in the future, if they wished very hard and followed their star, their dreams might come true. They spent their young lives being polite and articulate whilst the government lied and lied and lied to them again. They are not prepared to be polite and articulate any more. They just want to scream until something changes. Perhaps that's what it takes to be heard.

'Look, we all saw what happened at the big anti-war protest back in 2003,' says Tom, a postgraduate student from London. 'Bugger all, that's what happened. Everyone turned up, listened to some speeches and then went home. It's sad that it's come to this, but...', he gestures behind him to the bonfires burning in front of the shattered windows of Tory HQ. 'What else can we do?'

We're back at Millbank and bonfires are burning; a sign reading 'Fund our Future!' goes up in flames. Nobody quite expected this. Whatever we'd whispered among ourselves, we didn't expect that so many of us would share the same strength of feeling, the same anger, enough to carry 2,000 young people over the border of legality. We didn't expect it to be so easy, nor to meet so little resistance. We didn't expect suddenly to feel ourselves so powerful, and now – now we don't quite know what to do with it. I put my hands to my face and find it tight with tears. This is tragic, as well as exhilarating.

Yells of 'Tory Scum!' and 'No ifs, no buts, no education cuts!' mingle with anguished cries of 'Don't throw shit!' over the panicked rhythm of drums as the thousand kids crowded into the atrium try to persuade those who have made it to the roof not to chuck anything that might actually hurt the police. But somebody, there's always one, has already thrown a fire extinguisher. A boy with a scraggly ginger beard rushes in front of the riot lines. He hollers, 'Stop throwing stuff, you twats! You're making us look bad!' A girl stumbles out of the building with a streaming head wound; it's about to turn ugly. 'I just wanted to get in and they were pushing from the back,' she says. 'A policeman just lifted up his baton and smacked me.'

'We voted for people who promised to change things for the better, and they broke all their promises,' Tom tells me. 'There's nothing left for us but direct action. I'm not one of those black-mask anarchists, by the way. I just think this is right. This is what needed to happen. We needed to make ourselves heard.'

Tom invites me to join him on the sofa. With a slight double-take, I realise that this is one of the executive sofas from inside Tory HQ, dragged out and plonked in the middle of the pavement with the burning signs and the litter. 'Come on, sit down,' he says. 'If we're going to be kettled, we may as well get comfy.'

Suddenly there's a cheer. The boys and girls who have made it to the roof have dropped a banner to announce their presence. The sunshine glints off their faces; we squint as we peer up to where they're punching the air, shouting in triumph, dropping more banners and leaflets fluttering like ticker-tape in the sharp winter light. A young couple lean over the edge and begin to kiss and cuddle each other, and for a moment it's beautiful, we are beautiful, we can do anything.

Then behind the crowd, I hear another sound, coming closer. It's the sound of an ambulance.

TALKING ABOUT A REVOLUTION

24 November 2010

Outside Downing Street, in front of a line of riot police, I am sitting beside a makeshift campfire.[1] It's cold, and the schoolchildren who have skipped classes gather around as a student with a three-string guitar strikes up the chords to Tracy Chapman's 'Talkin' 'Bout a Revolution'. The kids start to sing, sweet and off-key, an apocalyptic choir knotted around a small bright circle of warmth and energy. 'Finally the tables are starting to turn,' they sing, the sound of their voices drowning out the drone of helicopters and the screams from the edge of the kettle. 'Finally the tables are starting to turn.'

Then a cop smashes into the circle. The police shove us out of the way and the camp evaporates in a hiss of smoke,

1. This column was written on my Blackberry, in half an hour, whilst hiding behind a bollard from the flying broken glass. When I was about halfway through, some little bastard snatched my phone right out of my hand, but others made him drop it. I felt at the time that including this information may have seemed rather petty.

forcing us forward. Not all of us know how we got here, but we're being crammed in with brutal efficiency: the press of bodies is vice-tight and still the cops are screaming at us to move forward. Beside me, a schoolgirl is crying. She is just 14.

'We followed the crowd,' she says. So did we all. There are no leaders here: the thousands of schoolchildren and young people who streamed into Whitehall three hours ago in protest at the government's attacks on further and higher education were working completely off script. A wordless cry went up somewhere in the crowd and they were off, moving as one, with no instructions, towards parliament.

But just because there are no leaders here doesn't mean there is no purpose. These kids – and most of them are just kids, with no experience of direct action, who walked simultaneously out of lessons across the country just before morning break – want to be heard. 'Our votes don't count,' says one nice young man in a school tie. The diversity of the protest is extraordinary: white, black and Asian, rich and poor. Uniformed state-school girls in too-short skirts pose by a plundered police van as their friends take pictures, while behind them a boy in a mask holds a placard reading 'Burn Eton'.

'We can't even vote yet,' says Leyla, 14. 'So what can we do? Are we meant to just sit back while they destroy our future and stop us going to university? I wanted to go to art school, I can't even afford A-levels now without EMA'.

I ask her who she thinks is in charge. Her friend, a young boy in a hoodie, grins at me, gesturing to the front of the kettle, where children are screaming 'shame on you' and throwing themselves under the police batons. 'Us,' he says.

This is a leaderless protest with no agenda but justice: it is a new children's crusade, epic and tragic. More fires are lit as the children try to keep warm: they are burning placards and pages from their school planners. A sign saying 'Dumbledore would not stand for this shit!' goes up in flames.

This is also an organic movement: unlike previous demos, there are no socialist organisers leading the way, no party flags to rally behind. The word spread through Twitter and Facebook; rumours passed around classrooms and meeting halls: get to Westminster, show them your anger.

Suddenly, there is a rush from the front and the sound of yelling police as hundreds of protesters run back from the lines, frightened. 'Don't throw anything!' implores a young, bearded protester with a megaphone. 'Protect your friends – don't give them the excuse!' But no one is listening. Sticks are being thrown: the mood is enraged as people see their friends struck back or struck down. 'Tory scum!' they yell. 'I wish they weren't breaking things,' says Leyla, 'but this is what happens when they ruin people's futures.'

INSIDE THE WHITEHALL KETTLE

25 November 2010

It's the coldest day of the year, and I've just spent seven hours being kettled in Westminster. That sounds jolly, doesn't it? It sounds a bit like I went and had a lovely cup of tea with the Queen, rather than being trapped into a freezing pen of frightened teenagers and watching baton-wielding police kidney-punching children, six months into a government that ran an election campaign on a platform of fairness. So before we go any further, let's remind ourselves precisely what kettling is, and what it's for.

Take a protest, one whose premise is uncomfortable for the administration – say, yesterday's protest, with thousands of teenagers from all over London walking out of lessons and marching spontaneously on Westminster to voice their anger at government cuts to education funding that will prevent thousands from attending college and university. Toss in hundreds of police officers with riot shields, batons, dogs, armoured horses and meat wagons, then block the protesters into an area of open space with no toilets, food or shelter, for hours. If anyone tries to leave, shout at them and hit them with sticks. It doesn't sound like much, but it's effective.

I didn't understand quite how bad things had become in this country until I saw armoured cops being deployed against schoolchildren in the middle of Whitehall. These young people joined the protest to defend their right to learn, but in the kettle they are quickly coming to realise that their civil liberties are of less consequence to this government than they had ever imagined. The term 'kettle' is rather apt, given that penning already-outraged people into a small space tends to make tempers boil and give the police an excuse to turn up the heat, and it doesn't take long for that to happen. When they understand that are being prevented from marching to parliament by three lines of cops and a wall of riot vans, the kids at the front of the protest begin to moan. 'It's ridiculous that they won't let us march,' says Melissa, 15, who has never been in trouble before. 'We can't even vote yet, we should be allowed to have our say.'

The chant goes up: 'What do we want? The right to protest!' At first, the cops give curt answers to the kids demanding to know why they can't get through. Then they all seem to get some sort of signal, because suddenly the polite copper in front of me is screaming in my face, shoving me hard in the back of the head, raising his baton, and the protesters around me are yelling and running back. Some of them have started to shake down a set of iron railings to get out, and the cops storm forward, pushing us right through those railings, leaving 20 of us sprawling in the rubble of road works with cracked knees. When they realised that they are trapped, the young protesters panic. The crush of bodies is suddenly painful – my scarf is ripped away from me and I can hear my friend Clare calling for her son – and as I watch the second line of police advance, with horses following behind them, as a surge of teenagers carry a rack of iron railings towards the riot guard and howl to be released, I realise they're not going to stop and the monkey instinct kicks in. I scramble up a set of traffic lights, just in time to see a member of the Metropolitan Police grab a young protester by the neck and hurl him back into the crowd.

Behind me, some kids have started to smash up a conveniently empty old police van that's been abandoned in the middle of the road. 'Let us out!' they chant. 'Let us out!' A 13-year old girl starts to hyperventilate, tears squeezing in raw trails over her frightened face, unable to tear her face away from the fight – I put a hand on her back and hurry her away from the police line. Her name is Alice and she is from a private school. 'Just because I won't be affected by the EMA cuts doesn't mean I don't care about the government lying,' she says, 'but I want to go home now. I have to find my friend.'

As darkness falls and we realise we're not going anywhere, the protesters start to light fires to keep warm. First, they burn their placards, the words 'Rich parents for all!' going up in flames, with a speed and efficiency gleaned from recent CV-boosting outdoor camping activities. Then, as the temperature drops below freezing, they start looking for anything else to burn, notebooks and snack wrappers – although one young man in an anarchist scarf steps in to stop me tossing an awful historical novel onto the pyre. 'You can't burn books,' he says. 'We're not Nazis.'

As I look around at this burned-out children's crusade, I start to wonder where the hell the student activists are. Whatever the news says, this is emphatically not a rabble led by a gang of determined troublemakers out to smash things for fun. In fact, we could do with a few more seasoned radicals here, because they tend to know what to do at demonstrations when things get out of hand. I find myself disappointed in the principled anarchists and student activists I know, who aren't here because they've decided that the best way to make their presence felt is by occupying their own lecture halls. I realise that these school pupils are the only ones who really understand what's going on: even people my age, the students and graduates who got in just before the fee hike, are still clinging to the last scraps of that dream of a better future, still a little bit afraid to make a fuss. These teenagers, on the other hand, know that it's all nonsense. They sat their school exams during the worst recession in living memory, and they aren't taken in by the promise of jobs, of education, of full lives and safe places to live. They understand that those things are now reserved for the rich, and the white heat of their rage is a comfort even behind the police lines in this sub-zero chill.

Smaller children and a pregnant woman huddle closer to the fires. Everyone is stiff and hungry, and our phones are beginning to lose signal: the scene is Dante-esque, billows of smoke and firelight making it unclear where the noises of crying and chanting and the whine of helicopters are coming from.

This is the most important part of a kettle, when it's gone on for too long and you're cold and frightened and just want to go home. Trap people in the open with no water or toilets or space to sit down and it takes a shockingly short time to reduce ordinary kids to a state of primitive physical need. This is savage enough when it's done on a warm summer day to people who thought to bring blankets, food and first aid. It's unspeakably cruel when it's done on the coldest night of the year, in sub-zero temperatures, to minors, some of whom don't even have a jumper on.

Some of them have fainted and need medical attention, some need the loo. They won't let us out. That's the point of a kettle. They want to make you uncomfortable and then desperate, putting your route back to warmth and safety in the gift of the agents of the state. They decide when you can get back to civilisation. They decide when the old people can get warm, when the diabetics can get their insulin, when the kid having a panic attack can go home to her mum. It's a way of making you feel small and scared and helpless, a way for the state's agents to make you feel that you are nothing without them, making you forget that a state is supposed to survive by mandate of the people, and not the other way around.

Strangers draw together around the makeshift campfires in this strange new war-zone right at the heart of London. A schoolgirl tosses her homework diary to feed the dying flames. 'I don't even know you, but I love you,' says another girl, and they hug each other for warmth. 'Hands up who's getting a bollocking from their parents right now?' says a kid in a hoodie, and we all giggle.

He's got a point. This morning, the parents and teachers of Britain woke up angry, in the sure and certain knowledge that the administration they barely elected is quite prepared to hurt their children if they don't do as they are told.

It's not looking good for this government. This spontaneous, leaderless demonstration, this children's crusade, was only the second riot in two weeks, and now that the mums and dads of Britain are involved, the coalition may quickly begin to lose the argument on why slashing the state down to its most profitable parts and abandoning children, young people, the disabled and the unemployed to the cruel wheel of the market is absolutely necessary.

Let the government worry about the mums and dads, though – I'm worried about the kids. I'm worried about the young people I saw yesterday, sticking it out in the cold, looking after one another, brave and resolute. I'm worried about those school pupils who threw themselves in front of the police van to protect it from damage, the children who tried to stop other children from turning a peaceful protest into an angry mob – and succeeded. I'm worried that today, those children feel like they've done something wrong, when they are, in fact, the only people in the country so far who've had the guts to stand up for what's right.

The point of a police kettle is to make you feel small and scared, to strike at the childish part of every person that's frightened of getting in trouble. You and I know, however, that we're already in trouble. All we get to decide is what kind of trouble we want to be in. Yesterday, the children of Britain made their decision, and we should be bloody proud of them today.

PROTESTING THE TURNER PRIZE

7 December 2010

In the low-lit central hall of Tate Britain, the great and good have gathered for Britain's most prestigious art award;

dealers and society belles are sipping champagne at black marble tables strewn with lilies, dressed in exquisite suits and designer dresses slashed to the thigh. The Turner Prize is an international by-word for gently baffling art, and its promotion of bland iconoclasts like Tracey Emin helped consolidate the self-reflexive iconography of the Blair era. This, believe it or not, was what radicalism in this country used to look like – but over the tinkle of piped-in piano music and wry discussion of ironic sculpture, a real cry of protest has gone up. Cordoned off behind two ranks of makeshift barriers, the young artists of the future have assembled to call out the hypocrisy of the rich.

Two hundred students from Goldsmiths, the Slade, St Martin's, Camberwell and other world-famous art and fashion colleges are intoning their demands in solemn unison, their voices amplified by the heavenly acoustics of the stone hallway into which they have been shepherded by the police. They mobilised via Facebook and Twitter to disrupt the Turner award ceremony in protest against upcoming government cuts to arts and humanities funding, higher education and public sector jobs. 'We are not just here to fight fees!' they yell. 'We are here to fight philistinism!'

The sound of their chanting rises psalmlike behind the police line, which has been tastefully boarded off by resourceful staff members. I'm not actually supposed to be here. When I heard that friends and comrades from occupations across the city were planning to disrupt the Turner Prize, I snuck in past the heavy security using the time-honoured journalist method of walking purposefully and authoritatively in the direction of somewhere you're definitely not supposed to be. I dash surreptitiously through the party and then dodge around the modesty screens separating it from the party, too fast for the security guards to grab me.

Suddenly, we're through the looking-glass. On one side of this screen, sullen middle-aged people have been made rich beyond their wildest dreams by exploiting popular nihilism; on the other, the age of apathy has ended as the trendy wing of Britain's disenfranchised youth reminds the wealthy that there's more to radicalism than pickling half a sheep in some preserving fluid. They are crammed into an alcove conducting what one dreamy-eyed young hipster solemnly informs me is a 'noise protest', shouting down Miuccia Prada as she awards the prize to a more gentle and considered sound installation.

'For too long, we were taught that our art could only reference itself endlessly, like a snake eating its own tail. But this is real,' says Margarita, 22, a media student at the Slade School of Fine Art. 'Ironic art is dead now – it's undead,' she says. 'That's because we finally have hope. We have something real, something to believe in again.'

'As an artist, this protest is a huge relief,' says Simon, another Slade occupier. 'That's not just because we have to stop the cuts to arts and the public sector, it's a relief because it's serious – the issues are deeply serious.'

Simon and Margarita belong to the generation that grew up in the apathetic nineties, when passion and idealism were unmodish and an ironic shrug the only authentic response to the rampant banality of consumer culture. But something has changed. For weeks now, the young British artists of the future have been occupying their departments in solidarity with the student riots taking place up and down the country, barricading the doors and abandoning their individual projects to work collectively on more practical art: banner-making and impromptu installations in vinyl and ink on the theme of capital and complicity. Meanwhile, delegates at the Turner Prize party munch on very expensive miniature snacks, cannibalising greasy crumbs of the caustic pre-crash self-reflexion industry.

Behind the screen, the children's crusade is screaming to be allowed some semblance of a secure future. On the other side of the looking-glass, as the well-heeled cultural elite of the Blair era drift in lazy pirouettes of ironic self-regard, the prize-winner, Susan Philipsz, takes a moment in her acceptance speech to defend those pesky kids that everyone had been trying so hard to ignore. 'Education is a right, not a privilege,' she says, 'So I support what the students are doing, I support the arts against cuts campaign.' I peek behind the police line just in time to watch the ironic smiles freeze into a group rictus of dismay.

INSIDE THE PARLIAMENT SQUARE KETTLE

10 December 2010

There is blood on my face, but not all of it is mine. I'm writing this from the UCL (University College London) occupation, where injured students and schoolchildren keep drifting in, in ones and twos, dazed and bruised, looking for medical attention and a safe space to sit down. It's a little like a field hospital, apart from the people checking Twitter for updates on the demonstration I've just returned from, where 30,000 young people marched to Whitehall, got stopped, and surged through police lines into Parliament Square.

They came to protest against the Tuition Fees Bill that was hauled through the House yesterday by a fractured and divided coalition government. They believe that parliamentary democracy has failed them, that the state has set its face against them. When they arrived at Parliament Square, they found themselves facing a solid wall of metal cages guarded by armed police.

Then the crackdown began and it was worse than we feared. As I write, a young man called Alfie is in hospital after a 'police beating' that left him bleeding into his brain, and all the press can talk about is the fact that a middle-aged couple – one of whom happens to be the heir to the throne – escaped entirely uninjured from some minor damage done to their motorcade. The government will no doubt be able to find the money to repair the royal Rolls-Royce, but yesterday it declared itself unable to afford to repair the damage done to these young people's future.

A kind father of one of the protesters has brought in a vat of soup; I'm slurping it and trying to stop my hands from shaking. Two hours ago I was staring into the hooves of a charging police horse before a cop grabbed me by the neck and tossed me back into a screaming crowd of children, and the adrenaline hasn't worn off.

Behind me, on huge makeshift screens showing the rolling news, reporters and talking heads are praising the police and condemning the actions of young protesters as 'an insult to democracy'. But when you see children stumbling and bleeding from baton wounds and reeling from horse charges underneath the glowering auspices of former prime ministers carved in bronze, when you see police medics stretchering an unconscious girl away from the grass in front of Westminster Abbey, her pale head swaddled in bloody bandages and hanging at a nauseating angle, you have to ask to whom the real insult has been delivered.

What I saw a month ago at Millbank was a generation of very young, very angry, very disenfranchised people realising that not doing as you're told, contrary to everything we've been informed, is actually a very effective way of making your voice heard when the parliamentary process has let you down. What I saw two weeks ago in the Whitehall kettle was those same young people learning that if you choose to step out of line you will be mercilessly held back and down by officers of the law who are quite prepared to batter kids into a bloody mess if they deem it necessary. What I saw today was something different, something bigger: no less than the democratic apparatus of the state breaking down entirely.

In parliament square, huge bonfires are burning as the young protesters in front of the horse lines at Westminster Abbey struggle against a new punishment tactic the police seem to have developed: crushing already kettled protesters back and down with riot shields. I find myself caught at the front of the line, squeezed and clamped between the twisting bodies of terrified kids, and my feet are swept from under me as the kids at the front tumble to the ground.

We all go down together, horses looming above us, baton blows still coming down on our heads and shoulders. I am genuinely afraid that I might be about to die, and begin to thumb in my parents' mobile numbers on my phone to send them a message of love.

On top of me, a pretty blonde 17-year-old is screaming, tears streaming down her battered face as she yells abuse at the police. The protesters begin to yell 'shame on you!', but even in the heat of battle, these young people quickly remember what's really at stake in this movement. 'We are fighting for your children!' they chant at the line of cops. 'We are fighting for your jobs!'

I struggle to my feet just in time to see a young man in a wheelchair being batoned. Disabled Jody McIntyre is dragged screaming out of his wheelchair when the police realise that photos are being taken, and shunted behind the riot lines as an even younger man who was pushing the chair shrieks, 'Where are you taking my brother?' Then, for some reason, the police decide to attack the empty wheelchair while Jody's brother is still steering it, perhaps in a cartoonish attempt to destroy the evidence.

The protest was never supposed to make it to Parliament Square. Desperate not to be kettled again, the young people who marched out of schools and workplaces and occupied universities all over the city veered away from several attempted containments and diverted into side streets, determined to make it to the seat of government to make their voices heard. When they got there they broke down the barriers surrounding the symbolic heart of the mother of parliaments and surged into the square for a huge party, dancing to dubstep, the soundtrack of this organic youth revolution. Besides the apocalyptic bonfires and thudding drums in the containment area, dazed and battered protesters share out rolling tobacco and carby snacks. 'Hey, look at this!' giggles one girl, 'I'm eating Kettle Chips in a kettle!'

This time, unlike the first three big days of action, there certainly is violence on both sides. While some students came prepared, even bringing a portable tea-and-cake tent complete with miniature pagoda to the kettle, others have brought sticks and paint bombs to hurl at the police. In the face of fellow protesters screaming at them not to 'give the coppers a reason to hit us', stones are thrown at horses as angry young people try to deter the animals from advancing.

Many of these young people come from extremely deprived backgrounds, from communities where violence is a routine way of gaining respect and status. They have grown up learning that the only sure route out of a lifetime of poverty and violence is education – and now that education has been made inaccessible for many of them. Meanwhile, when children deface the statue of a racist, imperialist prime minister who ordered the military to march on protesting miners, the press calls it violence. When children are left bleeding into their brains after being attacked by the police, the press calls it legitimate force.

Hanging off some traffic lights, my back aching from the crush, I have the best view in the house of this 'legitimate force' being enacted, as a line of riot cops forms a solid carapace of beetlish menace and marches forward into the crowd, raining down baton blows. Then the protesters cluster together and push back, and my mouth falls open as I see the police retreat into formation. I am suddenly reminded of school history lessons about Roman battle tactics, and indeed, looking down at my hands as I type, I notice that they are covered in blue paint and streaked with blood. It's clear who the Celtic warriors are in this equation.

When I drop down from the traffic lights, my arms and back aching from being crushed earlier, I find myself at the front of the riot line, being shoved between two shields. Fighting for breath, I am shoved roughly through the line by two police officers; twisting my neck, I see a young woman in a white bobble hat pinned between the shields and the crowd, screaming as the batons come down on her head once, twice, and her spectacles are wrenched from her face. Her friend is shrieking, 'please don't crush us, we can't move back, there's no room!' She is pushed through the line, too, and the police refuse to find her a medic. 'I've never been on a protest before, I'm a completely peaceful person – I'm doing my PhD on Virginia Woolf,' she pants, her face streaked with tears of anger. 'My name is Helen Tyson, and I'm disgusted, utterly disgusted by the police today.' We cannot speak any more, because a huge officer in full armour taps me on the shoulder and orders me to leave. When I explain that I am a member of the press and I'd like to observe what's happening, he tells me that this is a 'sterile area', and I am dragged away by my arms and legs and dumped by Horse Guards Parade.

A sterile area: that's what the heart of our democracy has become, a searing wound of rage and retribution cauterised by armoured and merciless agents of the state.

Things fall apart. Something fundamental has changed in the relationship between state and citizen over the past month. Increased police violence will not stop our democracy disintegrating: before it's too late, before more children are brutalised at the heart of what once pretended to be a representative democracy, this government needs to consider its position.

A RIGHT ROYAL POKE

6 January 2011

While children are having their heads broken outside the seat of government, moral knicker-wetting over the Duchess of Cornwall getting a light poke in the ribs is pure hypocrisy. After CCTV footage of protesters attacking a defenceless Rolls Royce at the tuition fees demonstration was released this week, conservative commentators have exercised themselves to the point of frenzy over the 'violence' of the scene, forgetting that the royals in the Roller weren't hurt, merely inconvenienced.

Unlike Charles and Camilla, many young people really were brutalised at that protest, in Parliament Square by baton-wielding police. Among them, 20-year-old student Alfie Meadows[2] was left with bleeding on his brain after receiving a baton blow on the head from an officer of the law, but his injury, unlike Camilla's gentle nudging, has not caused a national outcry.

Meadows nearly died on 9 December, but David Cameron has not condemned this assault as 'shocking and regrettable', nor called for the police officers involved to face the consequences of their actions. That night, as a barely elected government approved the effective privatisation of the British university system, thousands of students and school pupils were kettled for hours in the freezing cold, some hospitalised with broken bones and head injuries after being charged by police horses.

For a government unconcerned with such trivial issues as representing its citizens, however, the real violence that continues to be done to protesters opposing public sector cuts is of little importance compared with the symbolic violence done to the pride of the ruling elite by a smashed window and a few paintballs.

The Royal Family, it seems, are still entitled to tarmac-licking respect alongside their inherited millions. We may not be able to afford to fund further education for poorer teenagers, but by gosh we can afford a fleet to escort Charles and Camilla to the theatre in a Rolls-Royce. Unlike Meadows and other members of the public, the Royal Family still has a right to consider itself safe from public victimisation.

2. Alfie Meadows recovered from his brain haemorrhage. He has now been publicly charged with the crime of violent disorder for his actions on 9 December, presumably for headbutting a police truncheon.

As soon as that placard went through the window, so did all pretence of fairness on the part of the authorities. Within 24 hours, politicians were praising the police for their restraint in not actually shooting any of the unarmed teenagers who happened to run across the royal motorcade. This is to be expected: the sheer indecency of anyone daring to prod the future Queen with a placard is a breach of protocol so enormous that actual physical assaults on ordinary people are irrelevant in comparison.

The public purse can stand the cost of wiping some paint off a luxury car, but it is the symbolism of the act that matters. Alongside the Duchess of Cornwall, the entire web of hierarchical deference sustaining inequality in this country was poked with a stick on 9 December, and the coalition won't stand for that. A little jostling of the rich and privileged, however, should not outrage anyone with any sense of moral perspective.

What should outrage us is the fact that we now live in a country where symbolic acts carried out by angry teenagers who have just had their futures vandalised are considered criminal 'violence' worthy of national witch hunts, while battering peaceful protesters to a bloody pulp for daring to speak out is considered 'reasonable force'. If we truly believe in social democracy, such special pleading for special breeding should appal us.

NO SEX, NO DRUGS AND NO LEADERS

3 February 2011

It's just before midnight, in the damp chill of an austerity winter, and a gang of students and schoolkids is standing smoking against the iron railings outside an occupied lecture hall. 'All that aspiration was pretty much for nothing when there are no jobs,' says Amit, 18, a computer science student from Medway. 'This fight is so much more important than blind careerism. Just don't tell my parents I said that.'

It is the last day of November, and we are outside the Jeremy Bentham Room at University College London (UCL), the unofficial London headquarters of a national youth movement that has sprung up in protest at the government's cuts to higher education and welfare. Some of these protesters already have scars and bruises from the riot lines.

Behind the fire doors is a hub of light and activity. Amid the tangle of blankets and computer cables, students are sending out press releases, updating the group's Twitter feed and liaising with fellow dissidents about keeping the younger contingent safe on tomorrow's day of direct action against the tuition fees hike, which will involve tens of thousands of students and school pupils across the country.

'People have to stop talking about us like we're just idealistic kids,' says a girl in a grey hoodie, jabbing her roll-up in my direction. 'We're on the front line of a class war.'

Then, behind her, another shout goes up. 'It's snowing!' says one of the students, interrupting a debate on police brutality to rush over to the window. 'It's snowing!' These members of the so-called lost generation press their faces against the glass, or hurry towards the doors to go outside and catch fat, frozen snowflakes on their tongues.

These young people have been radicalised extremely quickly. At the riots on 10 November, it was as if a pressure valve had been released as thousands of students and schoolchildren broke away from the sedate march through central London planned by the National Union of Students, occupying the

Conservative Party's headquarters on Millbank, smashing windows and daubing slogans on the walls.

The anger and frustration that exploded at Millbank had been building quietly for years, as young people began to realise what a bleak future contemporary politics promises, and began to question if it has to be like this. 'I got involved after Millbank, because that was when I realised we didn't just have to lie down and accept these cuts,' says Jack, 30, a mature student from Gateshead. 'When we bailed out the banks, young people realised that capitalism had screwed us all. But after Millbank, the possibility of resistance became real.'

On the evening of 30 November, the realism that the girl in the grey hoodie observed kicks back hard. The latest protests organised by this diverse and decentralised network of young people run headlong into another round of beatings and arrests. Many students stumble back to UCL with bruises, bloodied heads and twisted arms after a breathless race through central London outflanking the police lines.

As the lost generation has begun to find itself, it has been met with brutal resistance from the authorities. 'Yes, it's scary,' says Tasha, a 16-year-old with a lisp and a tongue stud. 'But it's wonderful, too. It feels like something real is finally happening, you know?'

Finally, something real is happening – that is the sense you get as a young person walking into this space, stuffed with sleeping bags and suitcases and scattered schoolbooks, plastered with slogans and messages of support from around the world.

Everyone remembers their first protest march, so that romance is nothing new. What is new is the means of resistance – the tools, from Twitter and Facebook to auto-updating maps of the riot lines – that have carried the energy of this movement into the new year and beyond. These young people are idealistic, but they are also pragmatic, and they have the technology to build networks and share ideas quickly. The fight they've signed up for requires all three.

They come from all over the country, from across the world, and from different backgrounds, defying every stereotype of the privileged, white, middle-class, male student radical. 'I left school at 16 and worked in a carpet warehouse, and my political involvement was community volunteering – the 1980s recession never really ended in the north-east,' says Jack.

'Until Millbank, I used to think that student politics was just a lot of liberal wankers, frankly. But this lot really care about workers – they care about ordinary people, they're liaising with unions and community organisers. It's not just about student fees. It's about fighting the cuts as a whole, and insisting that education, job security and welfare support are every person's right.'

This is not business as usual for student politics. The polite institutional equivocation of the National Union of Students has been rejected. These activists prefer to hold more confrontational demonstrations – unplanned marches and attention-grabbing stunts that shut down big shopping centres and excite the global media. News of its impact is inspiring similar protests across Europe.

For most, politics used to be something that happened on television. Now, increasingly, it happens on the internet and everyone can be part of it. At UCL, the social networking machine is guided by two young men in their early twenties, and because both of them happen to be called Sam, they earn the monikers Techie Sam and Sam the Techie.

They spend most of their time huddled around a makeshift bank of computers together with a stream of helpers, coding, blogging and making sure that the various occupations and sit-ins across the country stay in touch.

The internet was supposed to make our generation apathetic and disconnected, but it has become a tool to turn back on the authorities, allowing us to make links and mobilise farther and faster than any previous cohort of radicals could have imagined, outstripping the sluggish machinations of mainstream political parties.

Techie Sam wasn't political two weeks earlier. A shy, stocky young man who looks older than 22 and professes libertarian tendencies, he got involved after his girlfriend, Jenny, was caught in the front line as police launched a horse-charge against student protesters outside 10 Downing Street on 24 November.

After Jenny was trampled and traumatised, Techie Sam realised that 'peaceful protest was no longer an option. I feared for my safety if I dared to go on the streets, so I decided to offer my particular skill set to the movement and to help in the way I know how.'

He now finds himself working so many hours a day that he's taken to sleeping in a roll of blankets under his desk in the room at UCL. It's not just Techie Sam. All of these young people are working hard, teaching one another about the best ways to resist police strong-arm tactics, putting their message out to the press and spreading the word: this is a resistance movement, and you can join in.

After a brutal police kettle in Whitehall on 24 November, in which thousands of children were penned like cattle in sub-zero temperatures, without food, water or shelter, for daring to speak up against the government's austerity programme, Greek students held a rally outside the British Embassy in Athens to express fellow-feeling. They were tear-gassed for their trouble, and many were hospitalised.

Back in London, students watched the live feed in horror. Three days later, they led their own rally to the Greek Embassy. A young art student from Athens – 22-year-old Margarita, dressed in denim, and a whizz with video installations – was persuaded to lead the British protesters in a chant of solidarity. She shouted a line in Greek and the Brits – the loudest of them a squatter with a thick Glasgow accent – chanted it back as best they could.

On the long journey home, Margarita was asked precisely what they'd been shouting. 'Oh, it's just something we say in Athens when the police beat us,' she said, smiling. 'It translates something like, 'Cops, cops, you're all murderers, we hope you die.' Members of the 'media relations working group' turned pale.

'I object to politicians using the term parliamentary democracy, because I don't think we have one any more,' says Ben Beach, 21, an architecture student who has been awake for 28 hours when we first meet.

'No one has the balls to stand up and represent the people they're meant to represent. We're about to be made to pay for a financial crisis that we had no part in creating. Education and welfare are being destroyed to pay for a £1.4 trillion bank bailout that wasn't our fault.'

Ben Beach is the Justin Bieber of the new left: a baby-faced riot messiah from Bethnal Green in east London with a tendency to hog the megaphone at demonstrations. He was trained in street activism by the Socialist Workers Party, making him one of a minority of student protesters with a background in far-left politics. It was Ben who, when the

Labour MP Jon Cruddas visited the UCL occupiers, pulled him up for speaking to the students as if they were not his ideological equals.

'Don't patronise us,' Beach told him. 'We're using an economic model that's based on debt – and that's why every decade we have a recession, each one worse than the last, and why every time the poor are hit hardest. The root of this crisis was the free market, and the only solution we've been given by any political party is more of a free market. Parliament is not addressing what caused the problems, and so society needs to.'

A similar view comes from Aaron Peters, 26, a former member of David Miliband's Labour leadership campaign team with a tendency to pull an Incredible Hulk act when out on protests. 'Parliamentary politics is basically over – it's dead,' he says.

On 3 December, as workers and students occupy and shut down Topshop's flagship store in central London to publicise corporate tax avoidance, Peters is quietly informed that he is, in fact, wearing a T-shirt from Topman. He immediately rips it off and stands shirtless on Oxford Street, stating that, even in sub-zero temperatures, one does not need exploitatively made clothes if one has the right ideals. Pictures of the incident later appear in the *Daily Mail*.

Peters and Beach are the sort of leader that this staunchly leaderless movement would otherwise have. Instead, the UCL occupation, and the movement as a whole, pursues a policy of consensus-based decision-making, an anarchist organising structure that gained credibility with the rise of green protest. Under this system, which involves hand gestures and autonomous working groups, there is no central leadership to report to. This means that everyone is allowed the chance to speak, and that the voices of women and younger pupils are given priority. It also means that direct action can be effected quickly, without any need for the bitter, arthritic infighting that blighted the student protests of the 1960s and, more recently, the Stop the War movement. 'They said it couldn't happen; they said that students could never mobilise like this,' says Peters who, thankfully, was fully dressed for the visit to UCL by Cruddas. 'Well, now we're everywhere. This is just the beginning.'

Clothes are a perennial problem. When Peters and Beach – who, like the rest of the gang, are quite prepared to get arrested if need be – stage a two-man protest outside a speech on education and the economy given by Gordon Brown at Bloomberg's London headquarters on 8 December, they need smart jackets to get into the event.

This is difficult because, after two weeks without hot showers, clean clothes or enough sleep, the members of the occupation have all drifted into a collective vagrant aesthetic. Eventually a three-piece suit is procured by way of a young man whom I'll call 'Peregrine', a barman and student at a local college who also happens – he reveals shyly in the third week – to be an aristocrat, which is why he is always asking everyone for money. Outside the Brown event, Beach gets a phone call from Peregrine. 'Um, Ben, you may want to check out that waistcoat before you go past security, OK?' Peregrine says. 'I think there's some acid in the lining.'

As I watch Beach frisking himself, as if his clothes were full of itching powder, a strange thought occurs. In a world where bankers can hold governments to ransom and where Tory ministers worship the free market with a cultish obeisance, these young nutcases may, in fact, be the sane ones.

Tellingly, the UCL protesters, unlike the 1968 generation with which they are so often compared, are – on the whole – drug-free, and have banned drinking at meetings and sex in the toilets. They don't want to ruin their reputation with a media machine that is already villainising some of their members. Besides, there is no time: they are too busy building links with trade unions, geeing up local councils and hounding Tory ministers outside public events, and some of them still have essays to write. These young people have been raised to work hard and play hard, and now they are turning that dedicated single-mindedness into a weapon.

Besides the merciful lack of dominance by a far-left-party vanguard, this is something else that differentiates these activists from the 1968 generation, and from those who fought Margaret Thatcher's reforms in the 1980s: they are in no way hedonistic or self-indulgent.

What shocks even more than the straight-edged sexual abstinence of the protesters, however, is the way this new politics affects how these young people relate to the world and to one another, working together, facing down the police together, sleeping huddled for warmth on cold floors.

On the morning of 9 December, the day of the Commons vote to triple university tuition fees, the protesters fumble out of their sleeping bags, pull on boots and woollens and prepare for battle with the police. It's going to be the biggest demonstration yet.

'People died in the 1980s,' Ben mutters. 'People might die today. We all know what's at stake.' There is a resolved silence as they pad their jackets with protective cardboard and scribble lawyers' numbers on their arms.

Peters calls for silence as Techie Sam puts a YouTube clip on the projector. A well-known actor's voice floods the hall, reciting from *Henry V*: 'We few, we happy few, we band of brothers / For he today that sheds his blood with me / Shall be my brother ... .' Ten hours later, many of these same teenagers will stagger back from the protest with blood running down their faces.

'Whatever happens now, everything has changed,' 23-year-old Sarah writes in her blog of the occupation. 'We've changed. Politics is the main topic of conversation. Demanding our rights has became normal.'

In the occupied college building, education is not a commodity, but an intimate weapon of social change, and Sarah seems to understand that better than anyone else. She grew up on a working farm in South Wales; she wears sensible fleeces and non-designer spectacles.

Only gradually, after spending time with the occupiers, do you realise that it is this soft-spoken geography student, not the more dramatic male activists, who is running the show, organising the meetings, making sure the younger ones are listened to. 'This is like a family,' is how Sarah puts it on the blog. 'That's the beauty of it. It's the sense that anyone can speak and be listened to; like any of these people I didn't know last week would come to my rescue if I needed it.'

That night, on 9 December, in front of a line of mounted police, as tens of thousands of protesters surge past the barriers into Parliament Square, I find myself standing next to Sarah, watching her throw up her hands to protect herself and others from a hail of batons.

Sarah's sensible fleece is flecked with blood, but she stands firm until the police run their horses into the crowd, pushing the protesters into a pen with nowhere to run. We stand until we are forced to the ground, crushed under a writhing, kicking heap of bodies. I grab Sarah's arm and we go down together.

Friendships always form quickly on the barricades, but this time a sense of solidarity is more important than ever. What is at stake here is not just the future of education in Britain – the catalyst for the protests – but a complete reconfiguration of the way young people understand civic society and their place within it.

Being born at the end of the 1980s was like rocking up in the small hours of a wild, destructive party and being asked to help with the clean-up, sweeping the fag ends off the floor and washing the stains off the sheets. We'd hardly arrived before Francis Fukuyama declared 'the end of history' and the final victory of liberal capitalism. This year, it's all changing. This year, Thatcher's children, the generation that was sold out and sold down from the moment we learned language, took a stand against the glacial creep of corporate oligarchy. In 2011, the eyes of the world are on Britain.

As the protesters hobbled back in from the kettle and headed home for the Christmas holidays, they promised to keep the energy going. By late January they were living in each other's houses, going to planning meetings every day, building links with trade unionists and workers' organisations that feel – in the words of Unite's Len McCluskey – 'put on the spot' by the student protests, which 'refreshed the political parts a hundred debates, conferences and resolutions could not reach'.

'This started as a protest; now it's a full-scale resistance movement against the cuts,' says Ben Beach. 'The difference is that protesting is just people objecting to something. Resistance is people saying, 'We will not let this happen'.

Frantz Fanon wrote that every generation must 'discover its mission, and fulfil it or betray it in relative opacity'. There is always the possibility that this generation could betray its mission; that the energy of resistance in this new movement could dissipate, dissolve into infighting, or be sold into quiet complicity. The leaderless, dispersed system of organisation, however, outstrips the traditional sectarianism of the old left, and selling out seems particularly unlikely: these young people, as they are constantly reminded, have precious little to sell.

Unlike the student uprisings of 1968 and the anti-globalisation movement of the late 1990s, there is no surplus of energy and jobs, and no easy careers left for these young people to escape into. Most of those who aren't already unemployed and outraged have no idea what they'll do when they leave school or college, apart from carry on fighting.

On 9 December, just before the tuition fees vote was lost, I saw a young woman standing in the crowd in the Westminster kettle, holding a sign that read, simply: 'Where's all this going to end?' The truth is that not one of us knows: this is an emergent movement, and with the stakes so high, the endgame is still obscured.

One thing's for sure, though: it goes far beyond a parliamentary battle over the Education Maintenance Allowance and student fees – the loss of those votes has, if anything, strengthened the resolve of the student protesters. Their struggle is about free education, but it is also about freedom itself.

This movement is redefining how politics is done in this country and across Europe. It is the pursuit of a politics that is not passive, but intimate and interactive. The mission is also persistence, but that won't be a problem. I am writing these last lines in a hall packed with new members of the movement, readying themselves for resistance days between now and March. 'We lost the vote,' says Jack. 'But we've still got everything to fight for.'[3]

WHAT REALLY HAPPENED IN TRAFALGAR SQUARE

27 March 2011

'We're fucked,' says the young man in the hoodie, staring out through the police cordon of Trafalgar Square, towards parliament. 'Who's going to listen to us now?'

It's midnight on 26 March, a day that saw almost half a million students, trade unionists, parents, children and concerned citizens from all over Britain demonstrate against the government's austerity programme. All day, street fights across London between anti-cuts protestors and the police have turned this city into a little war-zone. Barricades burned in Piccadilly as militant groups escalated the vandalism; the shopfronts of major banks and tax-avoiding companies have been smashed and daubed with graffiti, and Oxford Street was occupied and turned into a mass street party. Now, night is falling on the Trafalgar kettle, and the square stinks of cordite, emptied kidneys and anxiety. We've been here for three hours, and it's freezing; we burn placards and share cigarettes to maintain an illusion of warmth.

Commander Bob Broadhurst, who was in charge of the Metropolitan Police operation on the day, later states that the clashes in Trafalgar square began because 'for some reason one of [the protestors] made an attack on the Olympic clock'. That is not what happened. Instead, I witness the attempted snatch arrest of a 23-year-old man who they suspect of

3. As I write, in May 2011, similar waves of protests and street occupation have erupted in Spain.

damaging the shop front of a major chain bank earlier in the day.

It starts when a handful of police officers moved through the quiet crowd, past circles of young people sharing snacks, smoking, playing guitars and chatting. They move in to grab the young man, but his friends scrambled to prevent the arrest being made, dragging him away from the police by his legs. Batons are drawn; a scuffle breaks out, and that scuffle becomes a fight, and then suddenly hundreds of armoured riot police are swarming in, seemingly from nowhere, sweeping up the steps of the National Gallery, beating back protesters as they go.

Things escalate very quickly. In the space of a minute and a half, the police find themselves surrounded on both sides by enraged young people who had gathered for a peaceful sit-in at the end of the largest workers' protest in a generation. The riot line advances on both sides, forcing protesters back into the square; police officers are bellowing and laying into the demonstrators with their shields.

Both sides begin to panic. Some of them start to throw sticks, and as the police surge forward, shouting and raising their weapons, others band together to charge the lines with heavy pieces of metal railing, which hit several protestors on their way past. Next to me, young people are raising their hands and screaming 'don't hit us!'; some are yelling at the armoured police – 'shame on you! Your job's next!'

I find myself in front of the riot line, taking a blow to the head and a kick to the shin; I am dragged to my feet by a girl with blue hair who squeezes my arm and then raises a union flag defiantly at the cops. 'We are peaceful, what are you?' chant the protestors. I'm chanting it too, my head ringing with pain and rage and adrenaline; a boy with dreadlocks puts an arm around me. 'Don't scream at them,' he says. 'We're peaceful, so let's not provoke.'

A clear-eyed young man called Martin throws himself between the kids and the cops,[4] his hands raised, telling us all to calm down, stand firm, stop throwing things and link arms; the police grab him, mistaking him for a rabble-rouser and toss him violently back into the line. The cops seal off the square. Those of us behind the lines are kettled, trapped in the sterile zone, shoved back towards Nelson's Column as flares are lit and the fires begin to go out.

It would be naive to suggest that small numbers of people did not come to London today intent on breaking windows should the opportunity arise. It would be equally naive to suggest that no other groups had action plans that involved rather more than munching houmous in Hyde Park and listening to some speeches. Few of those plans, however, come to fruition: however the papers choose to report the events of 26 March, there is no organised minority kicking things in for the hell of it. Instead, a few passionate, peaceful protest groups attempt to carry out direct action plans, plans that quickly become overwhelmed by crowds of angry, unaffiliated young people and a handful of genuinely violent agitators.

Those young people are from all over the country, and when the word goes out at 2pm that something was happening in Oxford Street, they headed down in their thousands. By the time the 20-foot-high Trojan Horse arrives at Oxford Circus in the early afternoon, a full-blown rave is under way, coherent politics subsumed by the sheer defiant energy of the crowd. Chants about saving public services and education

4. There seems to be one of these at every protest, frantically trying to calm the crowd, and always with the same slightly Nazarene beard. Normally they get their heads kicked in for their trouble.

quickly merge into a thunderous, wordless cheer, erupting every time the traffic light countdowns flash towards. 'Five-Four-Three-Two-One ...' hollers the crowd, as bank branches are shut down, paint bombs thrown at the police, and small scuffles break out.

When UK Uncut's well-publicised secret occupation plan kicks into action at 3.30pm, the numbers and the energy quickly become overwhelming. As we follow the high-profile direct action group's red umbrella down Regent Street, we learn that the target is Fortnum & Mason's – the 'Royal grocers', as the news are now insisting on calling it, as though the stunt were a yobbish personal assault on the Queen's marmalade. The crowd is too big to stop, and protesters stream into the store, rushing past the police who are too late to barricade the doors.

Once inside, squeezing each other in shock at their own daring, everyone does a bit of excited chanting and then down for a polite impromptu picnic. Placards are erected by the famously opulent coffee counters, and tape wound around displays of expensive truffles imprecating the holding company to pay all its taxes. Tax avoidance is the ostensible reason for this occupation; the class factor remains unspoken, but deeply felt.

The posh sweets, however, remain untouched, as do all the other luxury goodies in the store, as protestors share prepacked crisps and squash and decide that it'd be rude to smoke indoors. When someone accidentally-on-purpose knocks over a display of chocolate bunny rabbits, priced at £15 each, two girls sternly advise them to clear up the mess without delay. 'It's just unnecessary.'[5]

5. The person responsible later offered to pay for the chocolate bunny in question. Nawwww.

Refined middle-aged couples who had been having quiet cream teas in Fortnum's downstairs restaurant stare blinkingly at the occupiers, who are organising themselves into a non-hierarchial consensus-building team. 'I oppose the cuts, I'm a socialist, but I think this type of thing is too much,' says property manager Kat, 32. 'There are old ladies upstairs. And I just came in to buy some fresh marshmallows, and now I can't.'

Outside the building, the crowd is going wild. Some scale the building and scrawl slogans onto the brickwork; others turn their attention to the bank branches across the road. I leave Fortnum's and make my way down Piccadilly under a leaden sky, past the ruined fronts of Lloyds and Santander, to Piccadilly Circus, where the riots – and make no mistake, these are now riots – have momentarily descended into an eerie standoff. The police raise their batons; the crowd yells abuse at them. No-one is chanting about government cuts anymore: instead, they are chanting about police violence. 'No justice, no peace, fuck the police!' yells a middle-aged man in a wheelchair. I scramble onto some railings for safety as a cohort of riot police move into the crowd, find themselves surrounded and are beaten back by thrown sticks. Someone yells that a police officer is being stretchered to safety. Flares and crackers are let off; red smoke trails in the air.

'A riot,' said Martin Luther King Jr, 'is the language of the unheard.'[6] There are an awful lot of unheard voices in this country. What differentiates the rioters in Piccadilly and Oxford Circus from the rally attendees in Hyde Park is not the fact that the latter are 'real' protestors and the former merely 'anarchists' (still an unthinking synonym for

6. He went on to observe that a nation beset by rioting faces a choice between chaos and community.

'hooligans' in the language of the press). The difference is that many unions and affiliated citizens still hold out hope that if they behave civilly, this government will do likewise.

The younger generation in particular, who reached puberty just in time to see a huge, peaceful march in 2003 change absolutely nothing, can't be expected to have any such confidence. We can hardly blame a cohort that has been roundly sold out, priced out, ignored, and now shoved onto the dole as the Chancellor announces yet another tax break for bankers, for such scepticism. If they do not believe the government cares one jot about what young or working-class people really think, it may be because any evidence of such concern is sorely lacking.

A large number of young people in Britain have become radicalised in a hurry, and not all of their energies are properly directed, explaining in part the confusion on the streets yesterday. Among their number, however, are many principled, determined and peaceful groups working to effect change and build resistance in any way they can.

One of these groups is UK Uncut. I return to Fortnum's in time to see dozens of key members of the group herded in front of the store and let out one by one, to be photographed, handcuffed and arrested. With the handful of real, random agitators easy to identify as they tear through the streets of Mayfair, the Met has chosen instead to concentrate its energies on UK Uncut – the most successful, high-profile and democratic anti-cuts group in Britain.

UK Uncut has embarrassed both the government and the police with its gentle, inclusive, imaginative direct action days over the past six months. As its members are manhandled onto police coaches, waiting patiently to be taken to jail whilst career troublemakers run free and unarrested in the streets outside, one has to ask oneself why.

Shaken, I make my way through the streets of Mayfair towards Trafalgar Square to meet friends and debrief. In the dark, groups of people wearing trade union tabards and carrying placards wander hither and thither down burning side-streets as oblivious shoppers eat salad in Pret A Manger.

By 8pm, there's a party going on under Nelson's Column. Groups of anti-cuts protestors, many of whom have come down from Hyde Park, have congregated in the square to eat biscuits, drink cheap supermarket wine, share stories and socialise after a long and confusing day.

'These young people are right to be angry. I don't think people are angry enough, actually, given that the NHS is being destroyed before our eyes,' says Barry, 61, a retired social worker. 'The rally was all right, but a huge march didn't make Tony Blair change his mind about Iraq, and another huge march isn't going to make David Cameron change his mind now. So what are people supposed to do?'

That's a tough question in a country where almost every form of political dissent apart from shuffling in an orderly queue from one march point to the other is now a crime.

'I don't have a problem with people smashing up banks, I think that's fine, given that the banks have done so much damage to the country,' says Barry, getting into his stride. 'Violence against real people – that's wrong.'

Minutes after the fights begin in Trafalgar Square, so does the backlash. Radio broadcasters imply that anyone who left the pre-ordained march route is a hooligan, and police chiefs rush to assure the public that this 'mindless violence' has 'nothing to do with protest'.

The young people being battered in Trafalgar Square, however, are neither mindless nor violent. In front of the lines, a teenage girl is crying and shaking after being shoved to the ground. 'I'm not moving, I'm not moving,' she mutters, her face smeared with tears and make-up. 'I've been on every protest, I won't let this government destroy our future without a fight. I won't stand back, I'm not moving.' A police officer charges, smacking her with his baton as she flings up her hands.

The cops cram us further back into the square, pushing people off the plinths where they have tried to scramble for safety. By now there are about 150 young people left in the square, and only one trained medic, who has just been batoned in the face; his friends hold him up as he blacks out, and carry him to the police lines, but they won't let him leave. By the makeshift fire, I meet the young man whose attempted arrest started all this. 'I feel responsible,' he said, 'I never wanted any of this. None of us did'

Back on the column, a boy in a black hoodie and face-rag hollers through his hands to his friends, who have linked arms in front of the police line. 'This is what they want!' he yells, pointing at the Houses of Parliament. 'They want us to fight each other. They want us to fight each other!

'They're laughing all the way to the bank!'

LIES IN LONDON

31 March 2011

As the dust settles and the slogans are scrubbed off the walls of Fortnum & Mason, that's the question the entire British left is asking itself about the events of 26 March. What went wrong? Where do we go from here? And most importantly, who do we blame?

That last part is easy: we blame it on the kids. The story currently being spun by the police, by parties in government, and by most of the press is that an otherwise successful mass demonstration was ruined by disgusting little vandals with hate in their hearts. That mindless acts of violence were perpetrated by a small, hardcore group of hooligans calling themselves 'the black bloc', who trashed banks and businesses at random and attacked the police without provocation. That their behaviour undermined and discredited the half-million citizens who marched to the rally point in Hyde Park. That it was a major own goal for the left in this time of crisis.

That assessment is incorrect on nearly every level. Unfortunately, the handful of reporters, including myself, who dared to produce accounts of the day that run counter to the mainstream consensus, have been savagely attacked. We have been called thugs, liars and terrorists for having the temerity to put on record the police brutality that some of us observed and experienced in Trafalgar Square. We have faced down attempts to bully and threaten us into retracting our testimonies.

I feel obligated to restate that the accepted public narrative about the events in London on 26 March is factually incorrect on several important counts. In the first instance, there were not a 'few hundred' dedicated 'criminals' on Oxford Street and in Piccadilly on Saturday, but thousands and thousands of people, mostly under 30 and unaffiliated, many of whom had come straight from flag-waving and banner-holding on the main march through Whitehall to join in with the peaceful actions planned in central London. These actions had been organised by the campaigning group UK Uncut.

Some of them, such as the store occupations, were potentially unlawful, but they were peaceful and politically motivated, like all of UK Uncut's previous projects.

Secondly, the 'black bloc' – a phrase that will undoubtedly be used to terrify wavering tabloid readers for years to come – is not an organisation, but a tactic. It is a tactic used, rightly or wrongly, to facilitate the sort of civil disobedience that becomes attractive to the young and the desperate when every polite model of political expression has let them down. Although there were a small number of genuinely violent agitators in attendance on Saturday, most of them middle aged, drunk and uninterested in the main protest, a great many of the young people who chose to mask up and wear black in order to commit acts of civil disobedience had never done anything of the kind before.

Those young people came from all over the country. They were students, schoolkids, workers and union members. Nine months ago, many of them were political interns, members of the Labour party or volunteers for the Liberal Democrats. Nine months ago, many of them still believed, however naively, that the democratic process might deliver real change. Now a new spirit of youthful unrest has been born into an ugly and uncomprehending political reality. A generation has been radicalised by the betrayal of their modest request for a fair future, and by repeated experiences of police brutality against those who chose to resist.

Those young people, with their energy and their idealism, briefly looked set to capture the hearts and minds of the nation. Following the events of 26 March, former sympathisers in the Labour movement and on the liberal left are now falling over themselves to disown Britain's disaffected youth.

Facing lazy calls to 'condemn the violence' or be held complicit in the media backlash, most of the centre-left has condemned, and condemned, and condemned. They have paused only to blame one another for ever entertaining these 'kids' and their politics. They have dismissed the angry young people of this country without actually asking themselves how it came to this.

That dismissal cannot be allowed to continue without serious unpacking. Ultimately, it is not these young people who have let down the Labour movement – it is the Labour movement and the Labour Party in particular that has let down the young, the poor and the desperate, not once but repeatedly, failing to stand behind their demands for change, failing to offer any alternative to the cuts other than its own re-election on a platform of slightly mitigated austerity. We should not be surprised that so many thousands couldn't be bothered to listen to Ed Miliband speak, and went to Oxford Street instead to do some direct action.

Then there's the third misconception. The 'violence' enacted upon the defenceless shopfronts of major financial fiefdoms may have looked terrifying and uncontrolled on camera, but it was far from mindless. These targets were not chosen at random. British banks and major tax-avoiding companies were attacked because these companies are seen by large swathes of the public as being responsible for the banking crisis and for subsequent ideological decisions on the part of the current government to mortgage healthcare, welfare and education. In the rush, Spanish banking giant Santander was also vandalised – and we need to be asking ourselves just what has made our nation's children so very upset with world finance that they believe any bank is fair game.

Nobody's children are at risk from this sort of political 'violence'. Many children were, in fact, part of the protest, singing and dancing on Oxford street or carried on the shoulders of their parents to watch UK Uncut's comedy gig in Soho Square. There are serious problems with the way in which the press chooses to discuss 'violence' in relation to the protests, and chief amongst those problems is the way in which the violence done to private property is now considered morally equivalent to physical violence against human beings.

It's the second sort of violence that really does put people's children at risk, and it's that sort of violence that I saw dispensed without mercy by police on the bodies of Saturday's young protesters, the vast majority of whom were engaged in peaceful civil disobedience, almost a hundred of whom were hospitalised for their trouble, with broken limbs and streaming head-wounds.

'The police tried to kettle us outside Fortnum & Mason, and fearing for the safety of the crowd in case of a crush, some of us formed a line in front of the police,' says Ben, 21,[7] whose face is swollen and covered in bloody cuts. 'This was passive resistance. Our arms were interlocked and we were clearly no threat to the police. Without provocation, an officer punched me six times in the face, hit me three times on the head with the edge of a riot shield, kicked me ten times in the shins and three times in the groin.

'I could not move or defend myself, so I bent my head to shield myself from his blows; it was only when I saw the blood running down my T-shirt that I realised how badly I'd been hurt.'

7. This is the same Ben Beach who is quoted in the article about the UCL occupation. He now has a permanent scar on his face.

'They were kicking people on the ground and dragging them away to be arrested. That was after blocking us inside the store "for our own safety" and promising we would be allowed to leave peacefully,' says one member of UK Uncut who was involved in the quiet sit-in inside Fortnum & Mason. 'We were handcuffed and taken to cells across London, made to strip to our underwear and given white paper jumpsuits to wear.

'I was left for 18 hours without food and woken up repeatedly, once for DNA swabs and fingerprints. It felt like they were trying to scare me away from peaceful protest, treating me like a faceless terrorist when I'm just an ordinary citizen standing up for what I believe in.'

Commentators are not wrong in calling 26 March a loss for the left. It is unfair, however, to blame that loss on the thousands of young people who chose to demonstrate outside the approved march route – although undoubtedly mistakes were made by organising parties in picking targets and anticipating the size and energy of attendance. The implication that the day would have been a success had everyone just played by the rules is a vastly disingenuous statement unworthy of the many respected liberal commentators who have made it.

After the event, Vince Cable released a statement to the effect that the March for the Alternative is to have no impact whatsoever on the speed and savagery of public spending cuts. The speed with which the statement was released strongly implies that it had been written before the first protestor had got on the coach. What 'ruined the day' was not young people committing acts of civil disobedience and spoiling it for everyone else. What 'ruined the day', if the day really was ruined, was the state's determination to ignore the weight of public opposition to its savage programme of spending cuts.

This is not to imply that the march was a waste of time, nor that those who marched were wrong to do so. Not everyone feels able to risk their job in order to occupy a bank. What the march and its aftermath reveal, however, is that the model of opposition and public mobilisation offered by the unions and the Labour Party is totally inadequate to the task at hand, and alienating for a great deal of workers and families, as well as the many thousands of people who are already too desperate to protest quietly and obediently.

Marching from A to B to voice vague objections to government spending plans, marching behind Labour and union leaders who fail entirely to offer a coherent alternative, is no longer a sufficient response to these cuts. It is not sufficient because this government, like the previous government, is not at all worried by the prospect of hundreds of thousands of people marching from A to B. They are worried about the prospect of a truly popular people's uprising. They are worried about losing the ideological argument over the necessity of destroying the welfare state. They are worried by the prospect of a run on the banks engineered by digital people power, as just occurred in Holland, and they are worried about the prospect of a general strike. It's safe to say that the government has a lot less to worry about this week than it did last week – and activists, anarchists, unions and the Labour movement all need to be asking ourselves why.

This government isn't scared of mass vandalism. The public, however, is – and that is precisely why fistfuls of images of young people in masks smashing up the Ritz and throwing smoke bombs have been tossed at our screens for five days now. The state requires us to be fearful so that it can acquire our consent for its spending cuts, and the public fears disorder even more than it fears mass unemployment and the decimation of public services. So perhaps we shouldn't be surprised that the images of officers of the law assaulting unarmed young people, and the images of riot cops arresting an entirely peaceful protest group on orders which are rumoured to have come right from the top, have largely been overlooked or dismissed.

Meanwhile, UK Uncut – a group whose modus operandi is inclusive, creative, defiant people power of the type that really does scare the government – has been brutally suppressed. In all 138 members have been detained, including a 15-year-old girl who was so frightened in jail that she was made to sign a form excusing the police from culpability, should she go on to commit suicide. There has been very little public outcry. The next wave in the battle for the hearts and minds of the British public has truly begun.

II
Girl Trouble

'Some people say little girls should be seen and not heard, but I say,
OH BONDAGE, UP YOURS! A-one-two-three-four!'

X-Ray Spex, 'Oh Bondage Up Yours!'

'Apparently this is the way one should be
Some clever boy said so, it feels fine to me...
So try not to see anything but the fee
It's all tongue in cheek anyway!'

The Indelicates, 'Our Daughters Will Never Be Free'

THE GULAG OF DESIRE

28 November 2010

You shuffle through the clinical, white foyer of the Olympia Grand Hall in Kensington and, after presenting several forms of ID to prove that you've paid the requisite £20 for your sexy times, security guards usher you into a huge iron stadium full of concession stands and bored-looking women in their scanties.

This is Erotica, 'playtime for grown-ups': a festival that is billed both as Europe's 'best-attended erotic event' and 'a unique shopping experience' – statements that, taken together, possibly explain a great deal about western sexual dysfunction.

If you had to build a prison for human pleasure, it would look like this. Among booths selling tacky, made-in-China suspender sets and a smattering of interestingly shaped dildos are concessions for discount bathrooms and homoeopathic Viagra substitutes; towering above the entire bazaar are giant inflatable female limbs, naked torsos and amputated legs in stockings suspended from steel girders a hundred feet high.

The punters are English, bourgeois and middle-aged; the strippers onstage and in the booths are young and eastern European. They smile desperately through shrouds of fake tan. The punters, a mixture of hardcore fetishists in rubber and older couples in fleeces, clutch plastic pints of lukewarm lager as they watch the grim stage show. Strippers gyrate in nothing but thongs and a couple of England flags, a cross between a jiggle joint and an Anglo-fascist rally. In true British style, the audience claps politely while pre-recorded applause thunders over the speakers.

I have lingered too long by the lube stand. A wolf-eyed salesperson in a company-branded T-shirt pounces, asking with rehearsed haste if I'd like to hear about the range of titillating products they have on offer today. Without waiting for an answer, he proceeds to test out a variety of intimate friction-reducing fluids on the backs of my hands. It's when he reaches the part about 'a nice, tingly, minty sensation all over your bits' that I lose the will to live. I back away, smelling of spearmint and sensing I've been violated.

By this point, I'm starving but the only nourishment that can be had here takes the form of gigantic hot-dogs: fat, grey phalluses, oozing chemical grease and waiting to be popped into polystyrene buns for a fiver. Ravenous, I buy one. It tastes rubbery and damply obscene, like an unwelcome intimate encounter. I tear into it vengefully. Behind me, the canned applause begins again.

Since puberty, I had wondered precisely what crypto-capitalism had done with desire. Like many randy young creatures, I always suspected that somewhere behind the welter of sterile posturing, the airbrushed thighs and hollow iconography of abuse, real sensuality was somewhere, straining for release. Now, I know. This is the Gulag. This is where pleasure is stripped down to its most profitable parts and flogged back to the middle classes at a profit. This is where sexuality has retreated, behind endless rails of overpriced latex. This is pleasure turned, inch by torturous inch, into work: the repetitive, piston-pumping moil of mass-produced erotic kitsch that passes for sensuality.

In a way, it's worse than work because we have to smile and pretend we're having fun. The *Daily Sport* girls in their booth have to smile. The rubber-clad dancers have to smile. Even the grey-faced punters have to smile, resigning themselves to a middle-age in which desire and satisfaction are gradually replaced by the purchase of more plastic tat.

At the end of the day, we all leave unsatisfied. Of course we do: if there were a single stall here where you could actually buy an orgasm, the whole edifice would collapse. It's the Gulag of desire. Nobody gets out, and nobody gets off.

IN DEFENCE OF CUNT

2 February 2011

It is, according to Germaine Greer, the one word in the English language that retains the power to shock. This week, after the third BBC newsman in two months – this time the revered Jeremy Paxman – dropped the c-bomb on live television, it appears that the world's best-respected broadcasting operation is in the grip of a collective and extremely specific form of Tourette syndrome, whereby presenters can't help but slip the worst word of all into casual conversation. One is reminded of those playground horror stories of cursed words, infectious words that, once read or overheard, niggle away in the forefront of your brain until, like poison, you're forced to spit them out, with deadly consequences. But what – ultimately – is so terribly offensive about the word 'cunt'?

The word shocks because what it signifies is still considered shocking. Francis Grose's 1785 *A Classical Dictionary of the Vulgar Tongue* defines 'cunt' quite simply as 'a nasty name for a nasty thing'. All sorts of people have a problem with 'cunt', even those who normally consider themselves progressive and enlightened: last week, for example, I was invited to speak at a public meeting where I happened to use the word in reference to a member of the audience.

Horrified silence fell in this roomful of hardened activists, followed a few seconds later by nervously appreciative laughter. The incident later exploded on the internet, with some complaining that I had had no right to use such a provocative and shocking word at a meeting; that the word is too aggressive, too graphic. These, for context, are people who are currently cheerleading calls for a general strike and/ or the overthrow of the government, but they still consider a young woman saying 'cunt' in public a little too, too much.

What is it about that word? Why, in a world of 24-hour porn channels, a world with Rihanna's 'Rude Boy' playing on the radio and junior pole-dancing kits sold in Tesco, is the word 'cunt' still so shocking? It's a perfectly nice little word, a word with 800 years of history; a word used by Chaucer and by Shakespeare. It's the only word we have to describe the female genitalia that is neither mawkish, nor medical, nor a function of pornography. Semantically, it serves the same function as 'dick' or 'prick' – a signifier for a sexual organ which can also be used as a descriptor or insult, a word that is not passive, but active, even aggressive.

There are no other truly empowering words for the female genitalia. 'Pussy' is nastily diminutive, as if every woman had a tame and purring pet between her legs, while the medical descriptor 'vagina' refers only to a part of the organ, as if women's sexuality were nothing more than a wet hole, or 'sheath' in the Latin. Cunt, meanwhile, is a word for the whole thing, a wholesome word, an earthy, dank and lusty word with the merest hint of horny threat. Cunt. It's fantastically difficult to pronounce without baring the teeth.

It is this kind of female sexuality – active, adult female sexuality – that still has the power to horrify even the most forward-thinking logophile. Despite occasional attempts by feminists such as Eve Ensler to 'reclaim' the word cunt as the powerful, vital, visceral sexual signifier that it is, the taboo seems only to have become stronger. Media officials avoid it with the superstitious revulsion once reserved for evil-eye words, as if even pronouncing 'cunt' might somehow conjure one into existence. The BBC wouldn't be in half so much trouble if James Naughtie had called Jeremy Hunt MP a 'prick' or a 'wanker' or a 'cold-blooded Tory fucker'.

For me, 'cunt' is, and will always be, a word of power, whether it denotes my own genitals or any obstreperous comrades in the vicinity. The first time I ever used it, I was 12 years old, and being hounded by a group of sixth-form boys who just loved to corner me on the stairs and make hilarious sexy comments. One day, one of them decided it would be funny to pick me up by the waist and shake me. I spat out the words 'put me down, you utter cunt', and the boy was so shocked that he dropped me instantly.

Ever since then, 'cunt' has been a cherished part of my lexical armour. I use it liberally: in conversation, in the bedroom, and in debates. I only wish I could hear more women saying it, more of us reclaiming 'cunt' as a word of sexual potency and common discourse rather than a dirty, forbidden word. If the BBC continues its oily pattern of vulgar logorrhoea, I'd like to hear Julia Bradbury saying it on *Countryfile*. I'd like to hear Kirsty Young saying it on *Desert Island Discs*.

Men have so many words that they can use to hint at their own sexual power, but we have just the one, and it's still the worst word you can say on the telly. Let's all get over ourselves about 'cunt'. Let's use it and love it.

WHAT *SUN* READERS SWALLOW WITH THEIR CORN FLAKES

17 November 2010

Page three, the pink and willing soul of British sexism, celebrates its 40th anniversary this week. For the benefit of the tender hearted, Americans and anyone who's been living in a box for the past 40 years, page three is the inside spread of the most widely read newspaper in the UK, the *Sun*, and since 1970 it has replaced actual news content with large, sweetly-smiling pictures of topless young ladies. Some humourless feminist types have taken issue with this, but these feminists are mistaken. Page three should be celebrated for what it is: a Great British Institution, like bad teeth, class war and golliwogs.

Complaining about page three can sometimes feel a bit futile. Its Identikit model of nubile, taut-breasted, blandly performative femininity has been part of the background noise of sexist iconography in this country for as long as most of us can remember. Slipped naughtily into our daily papers between the stock market reports and the body counts, page three normalises sexual objectification within the quotidian mindset of British neoliberalism in exactly the same way that unregulated trading and wars of occupation have become normalised.

For over 40 years, the *Sun* has served up a daily dose of military rhetoric and reactionary moral posturing masquerading as news, and it is significant that part of this propaganda explicitly panders to the assumed sexual fantasies of straight men. For the women and children who also read the *Sun*, the message is quite clear: not only that the proper role of women is to be young, naked and submissive, but also that the world of current affairs is geared towards the needs and desires of men.

Page three is far more harmful than any tawdry top-shelf skin mag because, without saying a word, it informs the millions of *Sun* readers who are not straight, adult men that the world is arranged for the social and sexual convenience of those who are.

Tits and bombs: that's the imagery *Sun* readers swallow with their Corn Flakes. Whenever one does complain about page three – asking, for example, that fellow commuters at least spare one from the pixelated titties – the retort is usually that the pornography is traditional, that it's just a bit of fun, and that humourless, unaccountably clothed women like oneself should learn to 'take a joke'.

'For any straight woman,' comments the comedian Josie Long, '9am is too early for tits.' However, taking issue with the daily assault of sexually objectifying images will invariably get one labelled as 'anti-fun', where 'fun' is synonymous with 'impoverished young women taking off their clothes and making a sexy face for money.'

To celebrate its 40th anniversary, the *Sun* launched a feature for the web – 'Page 360' – which offers *Sun* readers a new way to 'interact with their favourite Page 3 lovely'. Their definition of 'interaction' is rather special: 'simply click and drag your mouse and watch as she turns'. Some might consider this a bizarre interpretation of intimacy, but far be it from me to suggest that a culture that mistakes being able to manipulate a silent, naked, fake digital woman for actual human interaction has got problems that go far beyond any fiscal deficit.

It's all OK, because as well as being traditional and therefore unassailable, page three is a joke, tongue in cheek, and above all, ironic – although personally I've never understood the difference between an ironic erection and an unironic erection. Daily tits with the daily headlines are ironic, and hence not really meant or genuinely damaging. Sexual objectification as a part of neoliberal social conditioning is supposed to be a 'joke', and if you don't 'get' the joke, if you can't 'take' the joke, then it's your fault. Not all humour is equal, however, and a certain strain of 'joke' has always involved pointing and laughing at people who are less powerful than you.

Page three is this type of joke, and it's the type of joke that doesn't stay funny forever. It's funny in the way that black-and-white minstrel shows were once funny. Western society has a long history of expecting women and minorities to 'take' a joke in the way that one might be expected to take a punch.

We learn to take the jokes: we learn to shut up and smile. We shrink into ourselves until the blows stop coming. Unfortunately, every time I meet a woman or girl who has seen the dark side of sexual objectification, every time I meet a woman or girl who has been abused, battered, exploited or raped, I remember that some punchlines leave bruises.

THE SEXY WAY TO DIE

5 October 2010

A sickly pink rash has descended on the high street. Everywhere, push-up bras, patterned T-shirts and packets of crisps are festooned with rosy ribbons, drenched in sugary schmaltz, branded with the ubiquitous signifiers of slightly sexist sentiment disguised as popular altruism. That's right, it's Breast Cancer Awareness Month again. Buy these pink pants and you, too, can stand up to cancer – sexy, flirty, naughty cancer.

Every October, hundreds of charities and businesses across the world compete to bounce on the breast cancer bandwagon, 'raising awareness' of the disease with a series of perky pink products and a gamut of increasingly demeaning stunts. This year, the standard ladies' fun run in pink T-shirts isn't enough, so celebrities are lining up to join sponsored stumblers in stiletto heels, the idea presumably being that the best way to inform the public about cancer of the breasts is to make a complete tit of oneself.

Meanwhile, thousands of female social networkers have been encouraged to update their Facebook profiles with cryptic messages telling their friends where they 'like it': on the bed, on the floor, or possibly on the back seat of their brother's best friend's Ford Focus. This isn't the first time a frisky Facebook meme has used breast cancer 'awareness' as an excuse to drum up a little profitable exhibitionism.

In January, women across the world confided the colour of their underwear, apparently in the belief that playing along with yet another self-objectification fad might, in some arcane way, help the dying.

'Cancer is not pretty. It's not pink. And it's definitely not flirty,' wrote Susan Niebur in a letter to *Salon* magazine this month. 'It's a deadly, bloody, nasty disease, and it's killing me. Don't play games while I die.'[8] Many breast cancer patients and survivors and family members of sufferers have begun to take a stand against demeaning campaigns which seem to infer that breast cancer is serious not because it kills women,

8. Barbara Ehrenreich's excellent book, *Smile or Die* was inspired by her experiences of being told to think pink and think positive after her cancer diagnosis.

but because it threatens our uninterrupted enjoyment of lovely, bouncy, sexy boobies.

The products range from the cheesy to the downright threatening. One men's shirt sold in the UK warns women: 'Check your boobs – or I will'. In the US, the infamous 'Save Second Base' campaign has organised tight T-shirt contests for breast cancer – which, quite apart from being a staggering feat of point-omission, is in poor taste, considering just how many women have lost breasts to the disease.

All of this turns a profit for companies, while portraying breast cancer as a species of sexy lifestyle choice. In Breast Cancer Awareness Land, popular piety and the mawkishly totemic ribbons and bracelets of charitable one-upmanship combine with a rose-tinted refusal to acknowledge that, under our perky, plasticised, sexually performative exteriors, women have bodies that sicken, age and die.

All of this would be rather more excusable if the annual avalanche of pink garbage could be proved conclusively to be saving lives. Unfortunately, buying products with a pink-ribbon logo does not necessarily correlate with more money for research and treatment, as it is difficult to attach a tangible value to much of the corporate 'sponsorship' of breast cancer charities. In some cases, moreover, companies have begun to engage with 'think pink' rhetoric while making no effort to stop selling goods that may have contributed to the rise in breast cancer rates. It's a process known as 'pinkwashing'.

Uncomfortable as it is to admit it, the breast cancer awareness industry has become a gruesome global rehearsal of the collective capitalist fantasy that if we just shop hard enough, if we just buy enough junk, if we objectify women consistently enough, we can even prevent death.

It is perhaps understandable that cancer patients and their families should seek out a diverting routine of awareness-raising as a way of giving meaning to the prospect of what Susan Sontag aptly called 'an offensively meaningless event'. Yet big business is rather too content to cash in on the impulse. An event that sought to publicise an underacknowledged illness is now a multimillion-dollar scramble by commercial firms to turn grief and suffering into a cheerily homogeneous public experience – one that can be monetised and, in the process, emotionally neutralised. The facts of cancer have nothing to do with shopping, or stripping, or sexy stunts.

And until we have boring, unsexy things such as properly financed health care and a government that isn't determined to drain away science funding, this sugary-pink, boob-bouncing carnival of concerned consumerism will remain worse than useless.

VAJAZZLED AND BEMUSED

8 February 2011

Just when you thought that there was nothing more you could do to make your genitals more acceptable to the opposite sex, along came 'vajazzling'. The term refers to the burgeoning celebrity craze for shaving, denuding and perfuming one's intimate area before applying gemstones in a variety of approved girly patterns. The end result resembles a raw chicken breast covered in glitter. As the name implies, this one is just for the girls – nobody, so far, has suggested that men's sexual equipment is unacceptable if it doesn't taste like cake and sparkle like a disco ball.

Surely it can't catch on. Surely, no matter how ludicrous, painful and expensive consumer culture's intervention in our sex lives becomes, nobody is disgusted enough by their own normal genitals that they would rather look like they've just been prepped for surgery by Dr Bling. Or are they?

Suddenly, my teenage friends are popping off to get vajazzled. During the biggest shake-up of higher education in generations, someone at the University of Liverpool advertised a vajazzling evening for female members of the student body who really want their STDs to sparkle. All of this is sold as a fun, pseudo-feminist 'confidence boost', as if what women really need to empower themselves is not education and meaningful work, but genitals that resemble a traumatic, intimate accident in a Claire's accessories shop.

The beauty industry is constantly raising its already absurd standards for what constitutes an acceptable female body. Thirty years ago, plastic surgery was seen as the preserve of porn stars, actresses and the ultra-rich. Today, middle-class mums get their facial muscles frozen with botulinum toxin as casually as one might pick up a pint of milk on the school run; businesswomen take out loans for nose jobs and liposuction; and I can hardly turn around on public transport without seeing beaming adverts telling me how much happier and more confident I could be if only I paid a private surgeon to chop away at my healthy, living flesh.

Despite the downturn, 2010 was a record year for cosmetic surgery in Britain, including surgeries to help women's labia more closely resemble the plucked, blasted and sexless genitals of porn stars. Like vajazzling, labiaplasty is supposed to make one feel sexy but is a part of a creeping consumer war on sexual satisfaction.

What's most interesting about vajazzling is that it doesn't even pretend to have anything to do with pleasure. Most of the people I've spoken to who are attracted to women are bewildered by the idea of a vagina that looks like it's off to the Golden Globes without you. Vajazzling has nothing to do with sex and everything to do with the cruel logic of identikit, production-line womanhood, in which 'fun' means slavish adherence to the joyless motifs of corporate pornography and 'confidence' means submission to a species of surveillance whereby your nether regions are forcibly reshaped into a smile.[9]

It's all about making us feel that women's bodies – which are supposed to smell, leak and grow hair – are shameful and need fixing. As long as the beauty and surgery industries remain profitable, female sexual shame will remain big business.

BURLESQUE LAID BARE

15 May 2009

'Smile! You've got to smile until your face hurts.'[10] The director of our burlesque show didn't aim for subtlety. 'Smile in a saucy way, like you're thinking about giving them what they want. String it out. And then, when you do eventually give them what they want, keep on smiling.'

9. The Indelicates, 'Flesh', 2009 – 'Hey doc, won't you take my snatch, and scar it into a smile?'
10. Despite numerous pitches on less personal and more political topics, this article was the second piece I ever managed to get into a national newspaper, the first being the article below, about my experience of anorexia. I didn't want to write about my body for a living, but that's what newspapers seem to want from young women these days.

Four years ago, I was a miserable teenager, desperate for something to help me feel more at home in my body. After seeing a local burlesque troupe in action I was convinced that stripping was the perfect answer, and desperate for validation of any kind, I jumped at the chance. I wanted to rebel; I was enthralled by the dark, twisted aesthetic of the amateur burlesque I'd seen, and, just as importantly, I wanted attention, any sort of attention, to fill the emptiness I felt inside. There followed a year of making eyes and flashing my knickers, until my body felt even less my own.

Burlesque has been in the news recently, after Camden Council in north London decreed that burlesque clubs – like lapdancing venues – require an adult entertainment licence. This renewed the longstanding debate over whether contemporary burlesque counts as art or simply stripping. The council is clear, stating that any premises 'that wish to offer nudity, striptease or other entertainment of an adult nature will need approval from the licensing authority – burlesque falls within this criteria'. But Alex Proud, whose gallery has been forced to curtail its burlesque nights, has called the move nonsensical, arguing that such acts are not about stripping, but the apparently quite distinct 'art of removing clothes'.

When burlesque began in the nineteenth century, stripping wasn't even on the agenda. A form of low-budget theatre for the working classes, its main objective was to parody – or 'burlesque' – the cultural mores of the aristocracy. Early shows used comedy, music and dance to challenge the 'high-brow' art and politics of the upper classes, and made a daring mockery of Victorian gender norms by showing women dressed as men. It was only after many decades of burlesque in Britain and the US that women's bodies were used to help sell the art form to dwindling audiences.

Since its 1990s revival, burlesque has gradually shifted focus from social satire to simple stripping. This has been sold to the public as something subversive, even feminist – a democratic form of objectification which welcomes any woman, regardless of age or dress size. In practice, this seems to add up to the less-than-radical notion that women who have cellulite can be sex objects too. According to some, this is fantastic news for feminism, but 'body confidence' doesn't feature highly in my memories.

During the months of our 2005 run in Edinburgh, it was a rare day indeed when a shy, bewildered girl wasn't crying in the toilets backstage because she thought her costume made her look fat. Sometimes that girl was me.

In the past few years, burlesque culture has entered the mainstream, with hundreds of 'burlesque classes' springing up across the country. Polestars, one of the largest companies to run these classes, says they offer 'a chance for the modern-day woman to learn the old art of seduction and improve your body image ... to release your inner minx and use your femininity in saucy burlesque style!'

Peeling off my fluffy underwear in front of the Edinburgh crowds, it dawned on me that my headline act was no longer remotely challenging. Burlesque shouldn't have anything to do with your inner minx. Done properly it should be uncomfortable to watch – even terrifying. It certainly shouldn't be about reproducing gender norms, with women performing sexually, and submissively, for an audience. However, after I left, as my troupe became more successful, the managers ditched our most subversive acts. First to go were the cross-dressing, my favourite political sketch, and the reverse striptease (where a young woman ripped the

clothes off a male plant in the audience). What was left was
threadbare.

I began to realise that what really differentiated my act
from that of your average stripper wasn't the performance,
or the costumes, but simply class. Like the majority of women
who choose to get involved with burlesque, our troupe was
made up of middle-class girls, with the act offering us an
opportunity to indulge in raunchy exhibitionism without
feeling 'cheap' (at least initially). Burlesque serves up misogyny
in a tasteful package of feathers, while the explicit nature
of the shows increases each year. When I was performing,
complete nudity was frowned on, but burlesque acts such
as Satan's Striptease and Empress Stah have since started
offering full-frontal flashing.

Miss Roxy Velvet has been a professional burlesque dancer
for eight years. 'Certainly when I started performing, people
would do more unusual shows – really playing with gender
and politics,' she says. 'Maybe it's the circles I move in now,
but it doesn't seem to be like that any more. There are a lot of
burlesque clubs that are really oversexualised, really horrible.
And I think a lot of girls feel pressured to strip.'

At Roxy Velvet's show I watch a gyrating young woman
peel off her glittering costume as the audience whoops and
hollers, and I remember how intoxicating this used to feel.
Burlesque stripping, like lap-dancing, is about performing
– rather than owning – your sexuality. It's about posing
provocatively for applause. The transaction is one way: you
give, they receive. You pout, they clap.

The sexual tease, in all its forms, is a game that girls are
taught to play from early adolescence, and for many of us
it is the first real power we know. The burlesque striptease
makes explicit what push-up-bras and sticky lipgloss only

promise: a passive, faux-naive, peek-a-boo sexuality that has little to do with real female pleasure and everything to do with mimicking whatever we are told is 'sexy'. Sexual explicitness, on or off stage, does no harm to young women if it is combined with honesty, but burlesque has little to do with sexual honesty. It is part and parcel of the packaging of female desire, a process by which young women trade in their sexuality and their selfhood for whatever fleeting power they can grasp.

The day I hung up my stockings for good was the day I realised I wasn't interested in that sort of power any more. I prefer real power, power that involves my brain, that doesn't rely on tawdry male attention, and that will stay with me throughout my life.

The sexual tease is always a substitute for real personal and political power. In this respect, at least, contemporary burlesque is true to the spirit of the Victorian music hall, which plays on what historian Gareth Stedman Jones calls 'a culture of consolation'. In his essay 'Working-Class Culture in London', Jones identifies the nature of Victorian burlesque with a spirit of escapism, celebrating the small pleasures of working-class life as a compensation for social and political impotence. In precisely the same way, women turn to burlesque as a celebration of the limited, socially circumscribed forms of power that are permitted to us: the power to titillate, to excite, to look beautiful – all played out in silence. I became sick of being told that the stripping and grinding was acceptable, even empowering, because it was 'tongue-in cheek'. After months of being instructed to shut up and smile, I didn't get the joke.

Contemporary burlesque has ceased to be subversive; it is now just another part of our own modern, sexed-up 'culture of consolation'. Tired of fighting for equal pay, reproductive freedom and the right to walk down a dark street without fear, tired of being judged for what we look like rather than what we do, today's young women can be forgiven for wanting to play with the small amount of power we have. But stripping of any kind can only offer passive, cringing empowerment at best. The sexual power-play of burlesque strikes no great blows for feminism. All it does is make us feel, for the space of a three-minute striptease, a little bit better about the hand we've been dealt.

ME, THE PATRIARCHY AND MY BIG RED PEN

10 October 2009

I'm back from the Feminism in London conference, where there were tears, standing ovations, rants, arguments (one between me and a nutty racist apologist in front of about a hundred bloody people) and where, in Bea Campbell's words, 'a good old think' was had by all. My brain is buzzing far too much to give the event the full write-up it deserves, so that'll have to wait. Meanwhile, here's what I did on the way home.

Defacing sexist Tube adverts is something that's been pioneered by the feminist groups I've been involved with in London over the past couple of years, but somehow I never seemed to have a pen, or a sticker, or the nerve, at the right time. At the conference they were giving out free permanent markers, so I shoved a couple in my pockets. The last session on prostitution, rape and objectification made me chokingly angry, and as I walked back to the station the anger was still there. Anger on behalf of the women I spoke to who have been raped, abused and silenced, anger that my sisters and I still have to live in a world where rape goes unpunished and child abuse goes unspoken and women starve themselves to death in their thousands in order to take up less space, where girls are brought up to hate their bodies and service men and be quiet and say sorry and fuck when we're asked to and shut up when we're told to unless we want to be thought of as crazy fucking bitches stupid cunts whores slags, certainly not fit enough for Rod Liddle to shag after a few drinks, ha-fucking-ha-ha.[11]

And on this journey home, with all this rage and frustration boiling in my head, it just so happened that I saw one too many adverts trying to sell me painful, expensive surgery to increase my 'confidence'. 'All it needs is a little nip-tuck', the advert promised, next to a photograph of a woman with unreal breasts bulging out of a skimpy top and her head thrown back in a gormless grin like someone had shot her with a tranquilizer dart.

And I thought, hey, screw you. I've got a big red pen.

So I took my big red pen, apologising to the people I stepped past like the ridiculously English person I am, crossed out the slogan, and wrote 'This is not normal – fight sexism!' in big red capitals across the advert.

11. Rod Liddle, a prominent British columnist, had recently written an article ('Harriet Harman is either thick or criminally disingenuous', *Spectator*, 5 August 2009) declaring that Harriet Harman, the then deputy Prime Minister, was unfuckable (even after a few drinks) and therefore politically irrelevant. Harman faced many such vituperative, demeaning *ad feminam* attacks during her time in office, including from male MPs, who nominated her for a 'rear of the year' competition. I later met and interviewed Harman, and despite my many issues with her policies I found her a tremendously statesmanlike and noble individual.

God, it felt good. It felt good, and it felt naughty – naughtier than shoplifting did as a kid, and the rush was bigger and better and braver. It felt so transgressive. Everyone was staring at me. I was invading sacred advertising space! I was breaking two of our biggest taboos – one, you NEVER mention that there might be something more important to a woman than looking whatever is currently considered 'sexy'; two, you NEVER talk back to the adverts. Never. Not allowed.

Thrilled, I got off the Tube carriage and climbed onto the next one along, where I did exactly the same thing on two more adverts. I continued in this manner, with commuters muttering and tutting and one elderly lady giving me a big thumbs-up, until a bloke in his thirties sitting opposite me beckoned me over – crooked his finger and beckoned – and said – 'Come on, what's the problem, isn't it the woman's free choice? Can't she do what she wants with her money?'

I said: 'Of course she can. Just as I can do what I want with my big red pen. She's free to pay people to mutilate her and I'm free to attack people for trying to persuade me that I should do the same, or that my baby sisters should, or my friends. That is MY free choice, and MY free speech. And by the way, the woman in the picture doesn't really look like that; see that little halo around her boobs? Photoshop.' We screeched into the station, and I jumped off and onto the next carriage with a rush of blood and bile to my head, feeling suddenly powerful.

Because today I know something for sure about the free choice of the theoretical woman the apologists talk about, that theoretical woman who's glad she spent her money on cosmetic surgery rather than education or her financial future, that theoretical woman who just looooves to look good more than anything, that theoretical happy hooker without a care in the world, I know something about the theoretical choices of those theoretical women conveniently put forward by every patriarchal apologist I meet – I know that my choices are just as important as theirs. I know that the choices of the former prostitutes with PTSD who I met today and the choices of the thousands of feminists I know and the choices of the millions of women who would really like to feel safer and stronger in their bodies and lives, that those choices are just as important as any choice we might make to cut ourselves up to look sexy. And you know, I can live with challenging that choice.

By putting up adverts telling me that to feel confident I must look a certain way, for the purposes of which I must have surgery, the owners of these adverts are taking away MY choice to feel good about my body. But with my red pen and a little courage, today I took that choice back. And I feel more powerful, and more confident, than I have in a long time.

GALLIANO'S FASHIONABLE BELIEFS

4 March 2011

The fashion industry is a vacuous sausage factory that minces down the bodies of vulnerable young people, tosses in handfuls of unexamined prejudice and squeezes out glistening parcels of expensive self-hatred. There is also, as Hunter S. Thompson might have said, a negative side.

After an alleged anti-Semitic verbal assault by the Dior designer John Galliano in a Paris bar, an earlier video emerged of him ranting about Jews and women. 'I love Hitler. People like you would be dead today,' he tells two horrified women. 'Your mothers, your forefathers, would be fucking gassed and fucking dead.'

Fashion people everywhere rushed to check their hair before joining the chorus of dismay, almost as if racism and sexism were not the stock-in-trade of their industry. In fact, it is an open secret in high fashion that black and minority ethnic faces – alongside women whose ribs cannot be counted through their rattan tops, or 'fat mummies' in the phraseology of Chanel's Karl Lagerfeld – are not welcome. The few working black models accuse fashion houses of declining to hire them on the basis of skin tone – model agencies recently suggested that perhaps consumers just don't like looking at black people.

Diversity in fashion is going backwards. The recent fashion week in New York, one of the most multicultural places on the planet, featured 85 per cent white models, a proportion that has hardly changed in a decade. Recent high-profile campaigns have showcased white models in blackface, and when real black models do make it on to the pages of magazines, the airbrushing invariably lightens their colouring and straightens their hair into more marketable, Caucasian styles. Then we wonder why anxious teenagers across the world are using dangerous toxins to bleach the blackness out of their skin.

What should shock is not just the substance of Galliano's comments, but the fact that it took a man being caught on camera explicitly saying that he loves Hitler for the fashion industry to acknowledge a teeny problem with racism. The rabid misogyny of Galliano's outburst has hardly been commented on because, while most people now acknowledge that anti-Semitism isn't very nice, the jury is still out on institutional sexism.

The misogyny of fashion culture, however, exceeds its apparent conviction that any woman with the temerity to do more than silently starve herself is abhorrent. Silent complicity surrounds the rapes and sexual assaults that are routine in the industry. When the designer Anand Jon was last year found guilty on 16 counts of rape and sexual battery of models as young as 14, the only surprise expressed by fashion insiders was that his victims had dared to come forward at all.

The pearl-clutching piety of the response to Galliano's ugly outburst is a primer in tasteful hypocrisy. High-profile fashion colleagues eventually expressed discomfort with his viewpoint, if that's an appropriate term for the sort of drooling monologue normally delivered by a park-bench pervert with two hands down his pants. The problem with racism and sexism in fashion, however, goes far beyond one slurring fantasist.

THE PRINCESS CRAZE IS NO FAIRY TALE

5 May 2011

There is a princess in all our heads. She must be destroyed. As the press continues to glut itself on the Cult of Kate Middleton, businesses are cashing in on young women's insatiable lust for princess paraphernalia: fake tiaras and fashion handbooks play into the collective fantasy that one day, if you are beautiful and good enough, you too can marry a prince.

This saccharine tide of glittery pink kitsch began in the mid-1980s, amplifying a harmless daydream into a terrifying collective hallucination of good behaviour rewarded with royal privilege. Since Disney launched its Princess product line in 2000, aiming to get 'three or four' pieces of spangly tat into every girl's bedroom, the tide has become a tsunami. Disney

Princess is now worth £4 billion, the largest girl's franchise in the world, and the fairy tale doesn't stop with little girls: adult women, too, are playing dress-up, holding princess makeover parties and flocking to see Diana's wedding gown as it tours America, as serious female writers devote endless speculative column inches to the minutiae of Middleton's post-nuptial experience. Have we all gone mad?

Kate Middleton is the perfect modern-day princess, in that she appears essentially void of personality; a dress-up dolly for the age of austerity. The new royal facial muscles seem to be fixed with such permanence into that lipglossed rictus of demure compliance that when she opened her mouth to speak during the televised ceremony, I actually jumped. As it transpired, all she eventually said was 'I will', as if someone had tugged a cord through the back of that custom McQueen gown to activate a voicebox of ritual acquiescence.

For a fairy tale, it's startlingly unimaginative. Middleton's short journey from millionaire's daughter to Duchess of Cambridge has been awkwardly rammed into the rags-to-riches framework, with gushing commentators envisioning her as an everywoman who, by virtue of being pretty, unobtrusive and fashionably underweight, won the loan of a priceless tiara and a lifetime of comparisons to William's dead mother.

Middleton is hardly the girl next door, but the cult of princesshood is, at root, a cult of social mobility, a fantasy of class treachery whereby good little girls grow up to have their own maids and a butler. Popular children's books like Usborne's *Princess Handbook* have whole chapters on how to deal with the servants. This is the ultimate makeover fantasy, a fairy tale of frilly, sequin-encrusted self-improvement that just happens to involve rigid conformity to the rules of contemporary femininity: smile and be silent, be beautiful and rise through the ranks, and you will be rewarded.

The handsome prince himself, as Peggy Orenstein observes in her excellent book *Cinderella Ate My Daughter*, is 'incidental to that fantasy, a regrettable necessity at best'. Once the royal ring is on the royal finger, once you've 'nabbed' your royal, in the worlds of Sky's unmitigatedly disturbing reality gigglefest *How to Marry a Prince*, his part in the story is over, and the reality of married life figures not at all. This ruthless, mercenary understanding of relationships is hardly a positive model for young people.

Orenstein notes that princess-mania is understood by some parents as a safe haven from 'premature sexualisation': the Playboy bunny pencil-cases and Lolita T-shirts for which other children clamour. Princesses are seen as the more innocent fantasy, holding a virtuous edge over lollipop-licking, pole-twirling teeny-whoredom. Am I alone in finding the choice less than inspiring?

Young women are offered two polarised models of submissive, pseudo-empowered femininity: the princess and the porn star. This is a binary that has existed for centuries: virgin or whore, handsome prince or handsome pimp, which one will you grow up to fuck for fame and fortune? Today's spectrum of feminine aspiration is a short colour run from sickly, pastel pink to hot, sexy pink, with the occasional detour into bridal white. But there is a whole rainbow of experience out there for girls to choose from.

The princess craze is not just a failure of feminism, but a failure of society as a whole to respect and treasure its young women enough to offer them more than a frothy pink fantasy of Happy Ever After. There's nothing wrong with a bit of make-believe, but for little girls everywhere, there are

better dreams out there than just wanting to be as pretty as
a princess.

SKINNY PORN

11 January 2011

Another day, another dainty dead girl. The premature passing
of the French model Isabelle Caro from complications due to
anorexia nervosa is as tragic as it is unsurprising. Caro, 28,
was the face of the world-famous Nolita campaign, a poster
project designed to show dieting teenagers the horrific effects
of anorexia on the body.

After the campaign, Caro briefly became the darling
of the shock press. Modelling contracts poured in, as did
talk-show appearances and a book deal for her short, painful
autobiography, *The Little Girl Who Didn't Want to Get
Fat*. Being the 'face' of anorexia won Caro fame, praise and
attention – everything she had ever craved. Everything apart
from life and health.

When Naomi Wolf wrote *The Beauty Myth* in 1990, she
observed that the rising epidemic of serious eating disorders,
which affect an estimated 3 per cent of young women in
the developed world, was passing under the radar of the
global press. Twenty years later, anorexia has become a
global obsession.[12]

12. After this article was written, it emerged that there is a growing
    trend for hardcore pornography featuring obviously anorexic
    women. Most anorexics are unable to produce a sexual response
    (self-starvation kills the libido) – but like most commercial porn,
    'skinny porn' is about the erotics power, not pleasure. In some
    cases, girls were recruited to 'star' in these films directly from
    'pro-ana' websites and self-help forums.

One can hardly open a newspaper without reading another gushing interview with a teenager battling the disease, or turn on the television without seeing another gruesome documentary blithely illustrated with pictures of pouting, half-naked waifs, featured just before speculation over what Victoria Beckham didn't have for breakfast. The press might not admit it, but anorexia is in fashion.

The anorexia industry, for which poor Caro was briefly the mascot, is cynical idolatry masquerading as public concern in order to sell magazines. The anorexic has become the famished saint of late-capitalist femininity: beautiful, vulnerable and prepared to risk everything to conform to society's standards. Hers is a self-defeating rebellion against the sexist surveillance of patriarchal culture.

Over two decades of gory 'awareness raising', real public understanding of eating disorders has barely improved. Nor have treatment standards – more than 50 per cent of anorexics never recover. The poster campaign in which Caro was involved backfired spectacularly because it was based on the assumption that anorexic women starve themselves to look more 'beautiful', rather than because of any deeper trauma.

Naked pictures of her still appear on 'pro-anorexia' websites, which are designed to give 'thinspiration' to self-starvers. As the anorexia industry expands, people with less glamorous but equally destructive disorders such as bulimia nervosa and compulsive overeating are deliberately ignored – as are the many sufferers who happen to be male, poor, non-white or simply unphotogenic.

As a former anorexia sufferer, I have been approached to write the woeful story of my teenage illness, not once, but several times. I refused because the nation's bookstores are already overflowing with sob stories stuffed with grisly details of vomiting techniques. When I was sick, I used to read those books for weight-loss tips.

In a society where anxiety about consumption has become the defining collective neurosis, it is, perhaps, inevitable that the image of the anorexic should fascinate us. We are perplexed by the self-starver's ability to transcend the needs of the flesh and, at the same time, compelled by it. More importantly, the fashion for anorexia taps into an increasingly popular loathing for female flesh – and fear of female flesh is fear of female power.

One thing is for sure: the anorexia industry has little to do with concern for women's welfare. If we truly want to protect young women from the siren song of self-starvation, it's not enough to persuade them that 'skinny isn't beautiful' – we must communicate the conviction that all women deserve to take up space, to nourish ourselves, and to be large and imperfect and unashamedly powerful.

VIOLENCE AGAINST WOMEN IN TAHRIR SQUARE

8 March 2011

Right now, thousands of Egyptian women who gathered to commemorate the centenary of International Women's Day in the newly liberated Tahrir Square are being assaulted, harassed and brutalised. Not by Mubarak's thugs, but by the men who lately stood beside them as equals on the barricades. As I write, images and reports are coming through on Twitter from women fleeing male aggression in the symbolic heart of what is already being called the Arab Spring. Speak it aloud, let it ooze over your tongue: how bitter does it taste?

'During the revolution, women weren't women – they were simply Egyptians,' writes Egyptian journalist Ethar El-Katatney. 'They stood right next to men to liberate their country ... women will not – and cannot – go back to being silent.' It appears, however, that many Egyptian men would prefer their women to do just that – to shuffle back to their kitchens and stop demanding silly things like social equality and political representation in the new secular constitution of the country they have just reclaimed.[13]

Solidarity has been the watchword of this global resistance movement, but some men seem slow to understand what that word really means. One cannot reserve solidarity for members of one's own gender. The vomitous hypocrisy of turning patriarchal violence against one's comrades in the same space where you fought state violence together just weeks previously should be obvious even to the mobs of men and boys currently chasing women through the streets of Cairo. The impulse to exclude women from the cultural revolution taking place across the Arab world is clearly a powerful one indeed. The entirety of Egypt fought for democracy, but now its men have turned round and said: not so fast. This revolution was just for the boys.

The liberation of the world from tyranny and destitution cannot precede the gender revolution. On the contrary, the emancipation of women across the globe from the double threat of state violence and male violence ought to be the

13. 'In the early battles [women] had fought side by side with the men as a matter of course. It is a thing that seems natural in time of revolution. Ideas were already changing, however. The militiamen had to be kept out of the riding school while the women were drilling there, because they laughed at the women and put them off.' – George Orwell, *Homage to Catalonia*, 1938.

force that carries the revolution forward, trailing freedom in its wake. The presence of women, and particularly of young women, at the forefront of resistance movements across the world, has been expansively noted – but how will the world cope when these women demand their rightful place in the bedrooms and boardrooms and circles of power, equal to men on every footing?

How will the world react when the women who liberated their countries demand the right to control their own bodies and their own lives? Today, in Tahrir Square, we're getting a first taste of that reaction, as a joyful celebration of a century of progress for women across the world descends into violence and chaos. And yes, it tastes bitter; even from across the world, from a position of monumental privilege, it burns in the mouth like bitten-back rage.

Human beings liberate themselves by throwing audacity in the face of power. The revolutions in Egypt, Tunisia, Bahrain and Libya have taken the world by surprise, precisely because they demanded the impossible – the toppling of corrupt and despotic regimes that had clung to power for generations with the backing of western governments – but some demands are clearly a bridge too far when spoken in women's voices. We can fight the state together, but as soon as we turn around to fight discrimination and domestic violence, the passionate solidarity of men dries up like semen down a trouser leg.

If women had not sacrificed, demonstrated, struck, fought and demanded the impossible for over 100 years, we would still be treated as second-class citizens, denied voting rights and access to health care, considered the property of our male relatives and forcibly married to husbands who could beat, rape and brutalise us as they pleased.

Women and girls still face violence, marginalisation, harassment, political and social exclusion, discrimination and abuse across the world, in their millions, every day, merely because they are female. The first international working women's day, a century ago, recognised that the liberation of women and the liberation of the working class in the Bolshevik revolution and were two halves of the same equation. In Soviet Russia, that lesson was quickly forgotten. A hundred years later, the revolutionaries of Egypt are forgetting it all over again. We cannot let them forget; we must not let anyone forget.

All day I've been justifying why women still need an International Women's Day. I'm sick of having to justify why, while over half the human race still has to swallow daily discrimination and abuse merely on the grounds of gender, we haven't yet sat down and said thank you, sir. Women and workers are not free enough yet to be grateful for how far we have come. We must continue to make demands, impossible audacious demands, and we must never apologise, not even when men try to shout us down, or beat us down, or cut us down.

A century after the first International Working Women's day, we must continue to demand the impossible on behalf of future generations, just as our mothers and grandmothers demanded it for us. History requires no less.

ZIONISM, CHAUVINISM AND THE NATURE OF RAPE

12 September 2010

For months, feminists have been trying to untangle the complex knot of racism, imperialism and misogyny that is the Sabbar Kashur case, in which an Arab man was sentenced to 18 months' imprisonment for 'rape by deception' by a Jerusalem district court after he supposedly tricked a Jewish woman into having sex with him by posing as a fellow Jew. That an Israeli court could convict on such a charge – and that an Israeli woman could file such a claim in the first place – caused international outcry, seeming to illustrate a poisonous culture of prejudice against those of Arab descent. Compared to such a clear-cut case of racism, how could the disdainful treatment of one rape claimant by the press be of any significance whatsoever? Fresh details emerged this week, however, that seemed to throw an entirely new light on the case.

Extracts from the unsealed testimony of the woman, who cannot be named for legal reasons, reveal that she initially alleged that Kashur had forced himself upon her, leaving her naked and bleeding in a doorway, but the charge was changed to one of rape by deception following a plea bargain after the woman's sexual history was revealed. The victim, it is claimed, had alleged rape on several other occasions after being subjected to a lifetime of violent sexual and physical abuse at the hands of her father. She had worked as a prostitute, had fled to a women's shelter, and was so traumatised and bewildered that the prosecution were worried about putting her on the stand to face-cross examination about her past.

This changes much about the story – but nothing about its racist ramifications. Even if the victim herself could be conclusively shown to have told the entire truth about her experiences, this would not for a second change the fact that the verdict given by the Jerusalem district court was scored with ugly cultural assertions about race, religion and fear of miscegenation.

The judge in the case declared that the sex was consensual, but that the woman never would have agreed to it had she known that Kashur wasn't Jewish. He added that the state of Israel had a duty to protect victims from 'smooth-tongued criminals' who sought to defile 'the sanctity of their bodies and souls'. It speaks volumes about the relationship between racism, sexism and imperialism in Israel that a district court was quite prepared to convict on the basis that an Arab had defiled a Jewish woman's bodily 'sanctity' simply by putting his penis inside her, but unprepared to countenance the notion that a woman who had been abused by men throughout her life might have been telling the truth when she claimed to have been brutalised yet again.

I am a feminist of Jewish descent whose relatives live in Israel, and for whom the idea of a Jewish homeland from exile is not a concept of emotional irrelevance. For me, the case is a fascinating illustration of the way in which the chauvinism of contemporary Zionism has come to imitate the chauvinism of modern and ancient patriarchy. The central issue here is one of property and power. It is no accident that the word 'chauvinism', whose original usage meant jingoism or an inflated, bellicose sense of territorial nationalism, has since the middle of the twentieth century come to be synonymous with 'male chauvinism'.

Chauvinism is about territory and ownership. Zionist chauvinism, at its most extreme, sees the land between the Jordan River and the Mediterranean as the birthright of Israelis, property for the consumption and use of all Jewish people, and understands the personhood of individuals who happen to inhabit those lands as an uncomfortable side issue. Male chauvinism, at its most extreme, sees the bodies of women as the birthright of men, for the consumption and use of all male people, and understands the personhood of individual women who happen to inhabit those bodies as an unwelcome nuisance.

For racists and imperialists throughout history, the invasion and defilement of 'our' women by 'their' men has always been a point of paranoia. The idea of protecting English female 'chastity' from the 'lustful Indian male' had a significant influence on the policies of the British Raj, and the notion of the savage Indian rapist was used to rehabilitate barbarous reprisals by British troops against the native population. 'In some cases, even dating has been criminalised,' commented Dr Golbarg Bashi, professor of Iranian studies at Rutgers. 'What is the difference between lynching young black men in the southern United States on the mere assumption of having 'laid hands on a white woman' and criminalising a Palestinian man for having done the same to a white Ashkenazi woman?' she asked. 'In a similar way, the gender apartheid in the Islamic Republic of Iran obliges women to seek formal permission from the state if they choose to marry a non-Iranian.'

Few states which have juridically criminalised inter-racial intercourse have historically shown much concern for protecting the personhood of women from relentless and very real epidemics of male sexual violence perpetrated against them by men from of their own ethnic background, including husbands, partners and family members. Rape as a function and expression of male power in a chauvinist society has habitually been accepted where miscegenation has not.

In an interview, Kashur commented that had he been a Jew, the charge of rape against him might well have been thrown out. Damn straight it might – and feminists and anti-racists everywhere ought to ask ourselves why.

A MODESTY SLIP FOR MISOGYNY

29 May 2010

Slip away the modesty cloth of faux-feminist posturing over the veil, and you'll find an ugly skin of nationalism, male intolerance and misogyny.

Many articles on the subject, particularly those written by men, miss perhaps the most fundamental question about the veil debate. The question is not to what extent the veil can be considered oppressive, but whether it is ever justifiable for men to mandate how women should look, dress and behave in the name of preserving a culture.

Male culture has always chosen to define itself by how it permits its women to dress and behave. Footage recorded in 2008 shows a young member of the British National Party expounding upon the right of the average working man in Leeds to 'look at women wearing low-cut tops in the street'. The speaker declares the practice is 'part of British history, and more important than human rights', and laments that 'they' – variously, Muslims, foreigners and feminists – want to 'take it away from us'.

Never mind the right of the women in question to wear what they want or, for that matter, to walk down that Leeds street without fear of the entitled harassment made extremely explicit in this speech. This is not about women. This is about men, and how men define themselves against other men.

In the dialect of male-coded cultural violence, whether it takes place on a street in Leeds, in a Middle Eastern valley, or in the minds of a generation raised on sectarian squabbling and distrust, women are valuable only and always as a cultural symbol.

Some years ago I spent a summer on a ward for eating disorders, where I struck up a friendship with a fellow patient called Sara, a Saudi Muslim who wore the *hijab* and smoked Italian cigarettes. When we were well enough to walk in the hospital gardens, Sara and I would spend long hours talking about how other people always seemed to want to control how we looked. She shared with me the privations of compulsory Islamic dress, and I explained the pressure constantly to appear feminine and sexy that I experienced as a British teenager raised by atheists.[14]

As an experiment, we decided to swap clothes for a fortnight. Sara wore skintight tracksuits and her short, spiky hair uncovered; I wore an *abaya* with full headscarf that she taught me to fold and tuck. What was striking was that when we took trips to the shops in our new gladrags, both of us felt immensely liberated: our bodies were finally our own, hers to show off as she pleased, mine to cover if I wanted. For the first time since puberty, I felt that people might be seeing the real me, rather than looking at my body.

This flavour of freedom, which for some women is central to self-respect, is just as valid and important a choice as the freedom to go bare-legged and low-cut. A truly progressive western culture would respect both. But what European governments seem not to have grasped is that the freedom to wear whatever little dress we like is not every woman's idea of the zenith of personal emancipation.

There are hundreds of points of action that feminists across Europe would prioritise above banning the burqa, were anyone to actually ask us. What about increasing public provision

14. I have been trying to find out what happened to my friend for four years. She went by the name Sara Mohammed, but that was not her real name, as her father was apparently a Saudi official.

of refuges and counselling for the hundreds of thousands of European victims of sexual abuse, forced marriage and domestic violence, rather than focusing state efforts on the fashion choices of a minority of women who wear the full Islamic veil? After all, it's safe to say that any woman who is forced to wear a burqa against her will has problems that will not be solved simply by forbidding the garment.

It is patriarchy rather than religion that oppresses women across the world, whether it wears the face of an imam, an abusive partner or a government minister. The truth is that the way women choose to present themselves is still desperately political, in Islamic culture and wider society. The Islamic veil is definitively a threat to western values, and will continue to be so as long as the west continues to define its notion of freedom as a measure of exposed and monetised female flesh.

In seeking to restrict women's free choice to dress as they please, whether in a burqa, a bolero or a bin-bag, European governments are not protecting women but rather mounting a paranoid defence of their own right to determine what constitutes feminine behaviour.

CHARLIE SHEEN'S PROBLEM WITH WOMEN

31 March 2011

Those who are experiencing acute psychological and chemical breakdown are endlessly entertaining, especially if they are so overindulged that we don't even have to pity them.

'I am on a drug. It's called Charlie Sheen,' said Charlie Sheen, on an American daytime show. 'It's not available because if you try it, you will die. Your face will melt off and your children will weep over your exploded body.'

It's hard to tell who is more demeaned by the endless coverage of this millionaire sitcom actor's scag-pickled brain slowly dissolving into a soup of fizzing self-regard: the acting profession, TV audiences in general or the global press for being more scandalised by Sheen's drug habit than how he has brutalised the women in his life for years. Of course, while Hollywood loves a scandal, violence against women simply isn't scandalous. On the contrary: it is routine.

Slapping the occasional prostitute has long been part of the mythology of the Hollywood 'bad boy' and Sheen has earned himself a roguish reputation for shrugging off assault allegations. On one occasion, he accidentally shot his then fiancée Kelly Preston. Never mind, though: apart from his wives, many of the women who suffered at the hands of this giggling wash-up in his sleaze lair were sex workers, so they were probably asking for it.

Before Sheen started denouncing his employers across American news networks, he drew the attention of the press for 'cavorting with porn stars'. What appeared to shock prim media outlets, however, was not that Sheen had threatened a string of female sex workers but that he had associated with them at all. It's almost as if we still live in a culture that believes that women who trade on their sexuality in any way are asking to be beaten, raped and murdered. It's almost as if we live in a culture that believes that sex workers – and not the men who abuse them – should be ashamed of themselves.

When a celebrity who also happens to be a violent misogynist falls from grace, it is rarely the misogyny that draws comment. Last summer, when Mel Gibson finally tossed off one foaming racist diatribe too many, the entire press chose to ignore the context in which that rant was delivered – namely a terrifying outburst directed at his former partner, the mother of his child. Mike Tyson and other known rapists are treated as good ol' boys. They are portrayed as dangerous, exciting junkies who are not only cool enough to take drugs and smack women about but are wealthy enough to pay for it.

It is clear that, in the world of celebrity, terrorising women, especially if they are younger than you, poorer than you or sleeping with you, does not exclude you from becoming what Sheen deems 'a total freakin' rock star from Mars'.

When such people are already so chest-pumpingly high on the oxygen of publicity, it is hard to want to give them a single extra column inch. However hilarious their pop-eyed self-destructive benders, though, the violent misogyny of some of our smuggest folk heroes can no longer be dismissed.

THE SHAME IS ALL THEIRS

3 April 2011

The NHS is not a moral arbiter. Addicts, alcoholics and those who acquire injuries in gang fights and bar brawls are not required to justify their need for treatment before receiving it. The only patients who are obliged to make a moral case for referral to a doctor are women seeking abortions. Now, right-wing politicians want to go further and force women with crisis pregnancies to undergo counselling.

Let's not dignify this proposal with the term 'cross-party', since it's harder to get a spaniel to jump for a sausage than it is to persuade the Labour MP Frank Field to cross the floor. Pre-abortion counselling is already mandatory in many US states that have some of the most repressive restrictions on a woman's right to choose in the western world. The proposal by Field and Nadine Dorries would put the UK on a legal par with South Dakota, where abortion providers and the women they treat live in fear of murderous reprisals from Christian extremists, and which signed in a similar policy on 22 March.

The notion that abortion makes women mad has long been used to justify the withdrawal of termination services from desperate women 'for their own good'. The same argument has been used, within living memory, to excuse the imprisonment and institutional abuse of lesbians, prostitutes and 'promiscuous' females: it pathologises deviance from 'respectable' female behaviour as mental illness.

There remains, however, no scientific basis for a causative relationship between abortion and emotional breakdown. While there is nothing wrong with offering optional counselling to those who want it, telling women that they are 'bewildered' and risking their sanity, as Field and Dorries have done, is demeaning to the one in three adult women who do make that decision. Carrying a planned pregnancy to term can also be risky to a woman's mental health but this hasn't stopped the coalition government from slashing funding for palliative services for postnatal depression.

Some women do experience distress after terminating a pregnancy. That deserves to be acknowledged but so do the experiences of the many thousands of women who end pregnancies every year without regret. I have spoken to many women for whom the most distressing part of the process was waiting for the doctors' decision. Many felt ashamed to express the relief they felt after it was all over.

Forcing women to receive counselling before they can terminate their pregnancies would inscribe into law the notion that they are not mentally robust enough to have control over their bodies. The proposal adds to the already fraught process of accessing abortion services. It undermines the notion that women's sexual choices are valid.

Until we live in a country where sex education is fit for purpose and contraception is 100 per cent reliable, some women will need abortion services. Shaming women and girls who choose to terminate pregnancies – and enshrining their supposed mental incapacity in law – is both scientifically unsound and morally untenable.

III
Kingdom of Rains

'We live in a Kingdom of Rains, where Royalty comes in gangs.'
Montague Withnail, *Withnail and I*

UNDERCOVER WITH THE YOUNG CONSERVATIVES

8 August 2010

The teenager in the posh frock delivers her advice with the authority of weary experience. 'Since this is your first Conservative Future event, I thought I ought to say – watch out for the men here,' she whispers, as her friends disappear to the bar. 'Most of them can't be trusted.'

We're at the Young Britons' Foundation summer party, incorporating the leadership hustings for Conservative Future, where I've come to observe the young right in full victory rut. Descending three flights of stairs to the private function room at the Mahiki club in central London is a little like stepping into a sewer where the cultural overspill of the 1980s has been draining for the past 20 years. The room is stuffed with pasty young men in suits and ties drinking nasty orange cocktails and gossiping about Ken Clarke; the smattering of women present are wearing expensive polyester and listening prettily to what the boys have to say.

It's like a scene from one of those time-travelling detective shows, down to the droning muzak, the atmosphere of grim introspection and the suspicion that everyone here is acting a role. The young people lounging around the bar seem to be rehearsing a set of social stereotypes that feel too clichéd to be real, mouthing empty lines of propaganda – 'Thatcher did what needed to be done!' – with only a rudimentary understanding of their implications.

The Young Britons' Foundation is a finishing school for the centre right that claims to be non-partisan and offers classes in dealing with the media, but the organisers have somehow allowed at least one journalist to infiltrate an evening they're hosting for the youth wing of the Conservative Party. Eighty per cent of the people here are men and they have a lot to say about how the bloody Lib Dems are spoiling everything; and they say it over the heads of the women present.

'Yah, I really don't know what it is about Tory guys,' continues Posh Frock. 'They're worse than normal. I think it's because there are just so many men in the party and it makes them ... you know ...'. She fumbles in her bag, pulls out a pink gauze purse full of enough prescription medication to restock Boots and pops some painkillers. 'It just makes them arrogant, I suppose.' Is she some sort of feminist, then? 'No! God, no!' she squeals. 'No, definitely not, it's nothing like that. It's just – be careful. That's all I'm saying.'

A hush falls; the hustings have begun. The three candidates for the Conservative Future leadership are all boisterous white men in their mid-twenties, all tall, all a little jowly, distinguishable by the colour of their shirts and the fact that one of them is wearing hipster spectacles. Their pitches are a unanimous declaration of strategic befuddlement.

'Now that we're in power, we've got to show the left that we can win the ideological arguments because – because we're right!' declares Hipster Spectacles, but he doesn't sound convinced. His platitudes about 'progressive politics' elicit disapproving tuts from the back row, who seem to be conducting a rehearsal for their future in the Commons. 'Progressive, what does that mean?' mutters James from Kensington. 'Everything seems to be progressive these days. It's the buzzword.'

'Yeah, like the "big society",' enjoins prematurely balding Ollie, who works in the House of Lords and is slurping a Mai Tai from a tumbler shaped like a tribal woman's skull (my drink is in half a pineapple; it's all terribly ethnic).

'Nobody knows what the "big society" means! It doesn't mean anything!'

'It means cutting about a hundred billion a year from public services,' says his friend, adding hastily: 'I mean, like, obviously that's a good thing.'

'We need to make sure our party follows our principles and not those of the Liberal Democrats!' shouts another candidate. 'It's the bloody Lib Dems who're the problem. They're getting in the way of everything!'

During the bellow of assent that follows, one of my new friends brushes a hand surreptitiously and quite deliberately against my knee, like someone trying to be seductive in the seventeenth century. With a flash of awful clarity, I realise that these are precisely the young men my grandmother warned me about – that these are the heirs-apparent to Britain's political system, and not one of them has paused to consider if they deserve it.

The debate is thrown open to the floor and eventually one of the few ladies in the room puts up her hand to ask a polite question about the representation of women in Tory politics. 'Well, obviously I think women should be more visible in the party,' begins one candidate, grinning as a roar of appreciation goes up for his blokey innuendo. There follow some platitudes about how unfortunate it is that few women are taking advantage of this uniquely welcoming atmosphere to put themselves forward and assurances that 'positive discrimination' will never be a part of Conservative Future's way of doing politics.

It's all right, though – there's at least one woman whom these people respect. 'We need to attack the left like they attacked us,' says one of the candidates, his top button straining. 'We

need to vilify them like they vilified the greatest prime minister
this country has ever had – Margaret Thatcher!'

Sudden, thunderous applause and thumping of the bar from
50 young men in blazers who were largely prenatal when
Thatcher left Downing Street. 'She did what needed to be
done,' continues the speaker fervently. I begin to worry that
this is actually a neoliberal ecstatic cult, and that one of the
young men on the platform is about to start shaking and
summoning the spirit of the Iron Lady. Time for a little break.

Sucking down fresh Belgravia air and nicotine in the street,
I meet a young graduate in a pink shirt who decides to share
my lighter and his left-libertarian misgivings. 'The Thatcher
thing is weirdly sexualised, isn't it?' he says. 'I heard one of
them saying that it'd be a privilege to lick her boots.' It's
almost as if the right can't express respect for any woman
without declaring her super-sexy.

Unfortunately, despite my brilliant disguise of lip gloss
and vacant expression, Pink Shirt has recognised me as a
New Statesman writer. He promises not to expose me – on
condition that I go on a date with him next week. I decide
that, on a scale of one to patriarchy, this is likely to be the
high point of the evening, and accept.

Back inside the club, the debate has morphed into a disco
for the death of youthful defiance. Someone has turned the
lights down and the music up, and now the bright young
things of Britain's Conservative future are shuffling and
hip-swivelling to the Kaiser Chiefs, their ties at half-mast.
It's only 10.30pm and already there are several unfortunate
cases of gentleman's flush, the sweat-misted, red cheeks that
are the plague of the young right at play.

There seem to be a lot more women present, too. When
I ask the nearest person in tucked-in shirtsleeves why that

might be, he informs me that some girls 'just aren't interested in politics'. As if to prove a point, he grabs my arm and tugs me on to the dance floor. I wobble and totter like centre-right ideology on a pair of borrowed heels and, as Beyoncé starts to blast out of the speakers, I spin around in shock. I've just had my bottom squeezed.

Let me describe this bottom-squeeze to you, because it has given me lasting insight into the icy political libido of the young right. The anonymous fondle is brief, bouncy and strangely bloodless, like being groped by a Pete Waterman song. It's the sense of entitlement that stuns more than anything; the casual lack of respect for the less powerful, the assumption that it's all in good fun.

I knew that women and the poor were going to feel the pinch as soon as the Tories took power, but I never imagined the paternalism would be quite this literal. Unable to deliver a smack in the face for fear of breaking my cover, my knuckles or both, I do what women have historically done in any boys' club. I giggle and I say nothing. And then I leave.

BUNS, BUNTING AND RETRO-IMPERIALISM

27 April 2011

As the Royal Wedding slouches into being, Britain is drowning under a wave of retro kitsch. The boho wankers of London have decided that liking the monarchy is vintage chic, a bit like owning a Game Boy from 1991, and have emblazoned club hoardings with the slogan 'don't hate on Kate' superimposed over the Union Jack.

On the glorious day itself, a street party will be held in Shoreditch, in the heart of the capital's trendy art district, to celebrate all things British and bygone – like wartime 'victory rolls', the lindy hop and the relevance of the house of Windsor. This bric-a-brac of old-fashioned Englishness does not include a polio float or imprisonment for homosexuals, but there will be a Chas-and-Dave tribute band.

For some, this is more supporting evidence in the case for Shoreditch to be purified with fire, its juice-bars sacked, its art toffs and trust-fund junkies driven weeping to Camberwell and Newham where they may have to pay for their own drugs. The retro rot has spread beyond hipsterville, however.

Other street parties in the capital will be distributing T-shirts printed with the omnipresent 'Keep Calm and Carry On' design, the 'ironic' wartime propaganda poster that now infests the chinaware of the middle classes, reminding us that fortitude in the face of government-imposed austerity is just like fortitude in the face of Nazi invasion. As with the 'victory rolls', the message is confused: precisely what does the marriage of a young twenty-first-century aristocrat have to do with a war we fought 70 years ago?

Twee aesthetic nostalgia for a fantasy of 'lost Britishness' has reached fever pitch. It goes way beyond the wedding. A part of the *Daily Mail* offices is wallpapered with images of bulldogs, telephone boxes and, yes, Spitfires, done out in patriotic red, white and blue. Consumers are exhorted to buy dairy products on which, according to the advertisers, 'Empires were Built'. There is something monstrous in this fetishisation of wartime austerity and imperial pride, given that our government is currently dismantling the Attlee settlement and dispatching troops for yet another war of intervention – but there is something tragic there, too.

Inherent in this accumulation of cultural relics is the belief that modern Britain has little to feel proud of, and less to look forward to. Millions of people are about to lose their jobs and millions more are waiting for their living standards to drop through the floor as education, housing and basic consumer goods become harder to access. There is a sense that the future is closing down, while Britain's glorious past shines ever brighter.

The Second World War is reserved for special reverence, because this is the last moment in recent British history where we can be sure that our country was unmitigatedly on the side of good. Most of us want to be able to feel proud of being British, but that desire is being ruthlessly exploited in the quest for public acquiescence to enforced austerity.

The 'Blitz Spirit' is evoked by PR managers from Dalston to Downing Street, encouraging us to summon that deferential British ability to weather any storm our rulers happen to steer us into. What nobody mentions is that this willingness to Keep Calm and Carry On is one of the very worst features of our national character. All of this is no good reason not to take advantage of a day off and a party in the sunshine. But there is far more to Britain today than buns, bunting and retro-imperialism.

This country does not have to behave like a reclusive elderly person, polishing its relics in darkened rooms, hoarding mementos and paranoid prejudices from a time when the world made sense. This country doesn't just have a past. It also has a future.

THIS IS ENGLAND

29 April 2011

On the day of the wedding, this country is undergoing a profound identity crisis. 'It's generally felt that this is a time for serious politics,' says the young man in black, as police carry a battering ram and chainsaw past the smashed-in windows of his former home. 'The Royal Wedding is not serious politics. It's a joke.'

This is England in 2011: as the country gears up for the Wedding of Mass Distraction, police up and down the country have been bursting into squatted social centres and private homes, arresting anyone whom they suspect of having connections with the anti-cuts movement, on the pretext of preventing disorder at the happy event – sometimes seizing known protestors on the street or from their cars.

'It's a bit elaborate,' said one supporter outside the Ratstar squat in Camberwell. 'The police stormed the place at half past seven saying they were looking for stolen goods, but there aren't any here, we're doing nothing illegal. Now they've arrested eight people, and they won't let us take the dogs away.'

'Perhaps they're looking for leads,' his friend laughs, without humour. The police have, indeed, very little premise for these raids: different warrants are being used for every squat and social centre they burst into. No concrete evidence of conspiracy to disrupt the wedding has been found: despite the British press devoting weeks of coverage to these 'pre-arrests' and despite rampant speculation over the evil plots these dangerous radicals might be concocting to spoil the day, most actual anarchists in the UK couldn't care less about one faceless aristocrat marrying another. All that money and publicity poured into smearing the protest movement may have been better spent had Scotland Yard sent a hand-written note to every known dissident with the legend 'come and have a go, if you think you're hard enough'. The protestors, however, are refusing to play.

The excuse being used for the raid on the Camberwell squat is Section 8 of the Police and Criminal Evidence Act 1984 – or so the officer in charge tells me, but seconds later he dashes back to tell me that no, it's actually Section 26 of the Theft Act. 'It's nothing to do with the demonstrations,' he confirms. 'We search these places all the time. No, this has nothing specific to do with the demonstrations last year.'

'It's to do with the student demonstrations last year,' says officer U4570, nodding and smiling a few feet down the road. 'We're investigating stuff that happened this year and last year – the demonstrations.' Eventually, two or three officers admit that yes, the timing is to do with the Royal Wedding, saying, 'We've got to protect people.' Despite protests from neighbours, eventually all the occupants of Ratstar are arrested, and the royal couple can rest safe in the knowledge that they are being protected from cooking workshops and mother-and-toddler yoga sessions.

As squatters and anti-cuts protesters were being dragged out of their homes all over the country, pupils at my old alma mater, Brighton College – an exclusive private school on the coast – were celebrating Britannia Day. The entire school gathered on the north lawns for a picnic to mark the happy occasion of the marriage of one terrifying proto-royal automaton to another. Patriotic red, white and blue dress was mandatory, as was the case at many schools this week. So was participation in the college's first ever flash mob.

Yes, that's right. Flash dance events are apparently the done thing amongst the youth these days, and everyone wants to be down with the kids, particularly if they're trying to train them to run the country – so Brighton College decided that it, too, should have a flash mob. The college had arranged special hip-hop dance instructors to teach its pupils some groovy moves, and on a given signal, every proud member of the school, from the Master and prefects to the lowliest fourth-former, began to gyrate embarrassingly to the strains of 'I've got a Feeling' by the Black-Eyed Peas. In the rehearsal video, which was distributed amongst pupils to make sure everyone got the steps exactly right, two serious girls in leotards jive and thrust in an enormous private dance studio with studied, joyless grace. It is, without question, the whitest thing I have ever seen.[15]

This is a nation and a people undergoing a profound disturbance of identity. A few streets away from the Britannia Day celebrations, as the power of flash dance was employed to celebrate the Empire, more squat raids were taking place in Brighton. News was coming in about another, conveniently-timed swoop on student protesters connected with last year's anti-fees demonstrations. Since many of the men and women arrested and detained over the past few days have been known to the police for months, and few new charges have been upheld, the timing seems curious. The effect created is a narrative whereby the police are on one side, bravely protecting the royal family, the Union Jack, bunting, teacakes and traditional flag-waving deference, and on the other side is a mysterious army of dangerous yobs who deserve to be arrested for any crimes they might possibly be thinking about committing. We have become a country where protesters are 'pre-arrested' before they have a chance to make a fuss.

Some of the charges seemed spiteful to the point of poking fun. Among those charged with Violent Disorder for actions

15. My littlest sister, who was still studying at Brighton College at the time, attended the festivities decked out in solemn black, accessorised with our Nanna's funeral veil, in mourning for British democracy. The kids are all right.

on 9 December was Alfie Meadows – the shy 20-year-old student who, on that same day, was beaten so badly during a police charge that he was left comatose and bleeding into his brain. The sentencing guidelines for Violent Disorder note that 'it is not only the precise nature of the individual acts, but also the fact that individuals have taken part [in a protest]'. If there's a rowdy demo and you happen to be there, you can now be criminalised. 'We can protect you, William and Kate,' ran the *Evening Standard* headline that morning.

Back outside the Ratstar squat, plain-clothes police officers with spotter cards moved in and began seizing people from the crowd, arresting them on unspecified charges related to the TUC demonstration on 26 March. The assembled supporters scattered: I had seen enough, and got on a bus back through central London.

On Regent Street, I walked home under a parade of enormous Union Jacks decked out with military precision. Every shop window was festooned with more flags, congratulatory dioramas of clothes and accessories celebrating the coming royal union. Groups of revellers dressed in shiny plastic Union Jack hats were hurrying towards Westminster Abbey to secure their prime spots. Having just seen several people arrested for crimes they had not yet committed, I felt like I was in a scene from the film *V for Vendetta*, and recalled Chancellor Sutler's barking mantra: England Prevails.

Last night, mounted police charged on residents in the Stokes Croft area of Bristol, another hotbed of carrot-growing alternative living. This morning, as dignitaries and delegates gather from across the world to congratulate Wills and Kate, Westminster is a sea of flags. The story is a simple one of patriotism clashing with anarchism, and on both sides, the story feels forced. The real indifference of the protest movement to the wedding is mirrored by the real indifference of the majority of the population: a ComRes poll last week found that 70 per cent say they either don't care or aren't excited.

Most of us, whilst enjoying a day off, are disinterested in the lassitudes of this fairy-tale farce, the pomp and circumstance of the ceremony, the cargo-cult pretence of Business as Usual in Britain. Most of our real lives are about to get a lot worse, as the public sector is decimated, as unemployment continues to rise and the economy slides towards another crisis. Most of us are under no illusion of a happy-ever-after, and not just because we remember what happened to Diana. We know that something is deeply wrong with this country.

So this is England, on 29 April 2011. The marriage of the heir to an archaic and largely powerless royal dynasty is celebrated with pomp and circumstance, whilst dissent of any kind is suppressed on the smallest pretext, or none. If you step outside the system, if you refuse to stand and shout hurrah, if you question the narrative of easy privilege, if you offer an alternative or try to live one, you are a dangerous freak and you will be punished. The poor get poorer. The rich get richer. And England Prevails.

POPPY DAY IS THE OPIUM OF THE PEOPLE

7 November 2010

On a rainy Thursday in Cheshire, at a base belonging to Europe's largest arms dealer, veterans laid down paper poppies in memory of fallen soldiers. This was no protest, however: BAE systems, a prominent supporter of the Royal British Legion's annual Poppy Appeal, cheerfully hosted the solemn ceremony to mark the beginning of the Appeal at its Radway Green facility.

Officials from the arms and munitions company, which rakes in billions from international wars and is subsidised by the British government, watched as servicemen and schoolchildren planted crosses in front of the base. The awkwardness of their presence passed unnoticed in a country that seems to have fundamentally misunderstood the nature of remembrance.

It might seem a little disrespectful to describe Remembrance Sunday and the rash of poppies that precedes it as 'just show business', but that is precisely how Harry Patch, the final survivor of the 1914–18 war, characterised the ceremonies in his memoir, *The Last Fighting Tommy*. Patch died in 2009 at the age of 111; there is now nobody left living who truly remembers the futility of the war that sustains our patriotic imagination. Remembrance Day has been expanded to commemorate all fallen British servicemen and women, but in practice the events of the day focus on the two World Wars – and no wonder.

British children are raised on the mythology of those wars, in part because, particularly in the case of the Second World War, there were clear moral and practical reasons why conflict was unavoidable, and more to the point, we won. Neither of these things can be said of the desert wars currently providing BAE with a healthy market for their wares. Soaked in the powerful narrative of righteous heroism, the poppy of remembrance has become a fig-leaf for the overseas military interests of successive governments.

There are good reasons to donate to the Royal British Legion, especially with government support for veterans so notoriously constipated, but poppy-wearing, especially by public officials, is tainted with hypocrisy. The poppy was chosen as a euphemistic symbol of the horrors of war by a generation for whom those horrors were all too immediate; it should be doubly offensive, then, that almost a century later members of the British administration wear poppies while sending young people to fight and die far from home for causes they barely comprehend.

It is understandable that friends and relatives of the fallen might wish to find meaning and purpose in the offensive futility of war. It is unforgivable that governments and businesses should seek to do the same. It behoves our leaders to be mindful of the ugly, unsentimental nature of conflict, but instead the mounting death toll is listed with precisely the sort of macabre piety that horrified Private Patch. When the human wastage of a body count becomes an emotional excuse for continuing a military offensive, in order to properly honour the fallen it's time to question our attitudes to war.

'Sacrifice' is the word continually used to associate this cynical and relentless carnage with public nostalgia for the glory of past victories. There are, however, two meanings to the word. One can sacrifice, in the sense of willingly giving one's life for a cause, or one can be a sacrifice, offered up for slaughter by one's betters in the name of God, or greed, or homeland. It is this second understanding of sacrifice that we should bear in mind this poppy day. Even in the First World War, not all of the men and boys shot by their own side for cowardice or driven out 'like cattle', in Wilfred Owen's words, in front of the German machine guns, died with future generations in mind. Not all of them bled willingly, for king and country; some of them simply bled because they had been seriously injured, because their leaders deemed it appropriate for them to die in pain and terror. A million paper flowers, rooted in the dark earth of this country's frantic military self-fashioning, will never be enough to mop up the carnage.

Of course, there are those for whom the paper poppy is undesirable by virtue of being rather too declasse. If you're one of them, you might consider going all out and purchasing a poppy pin encrusted with Swarovski crystals, as Simon Cowell and Cheryl Cole have just done. What more fashionable way could there be to pay tribute to the unnecessary slaughter of millions than with a sparkly bit of political bling?

As we celebrate another Remembrance Sunday, we should remember that the politicians wearing red flowers in Whitehall have cheerfully authorised the decimation of jobs, welfare and public education in order to defend Britain's military spending and nuclear arsenal and offer tax breaks for business. They have sacrificed the life chances of a generation of young and working-class people while making rhetorical sops towards 'the national interest', and that is not remembrance, nor is it any way to honour the memory of the Great Generation. That, in fact, is 'just show business'.

MICHAEL GOVE AND THE IMPERIALISTS

1 June 2010

The Tories want our children to be proud of Britain's imperial past. When the right-wing colonial historian Niall Ferguson told the Hay Festival last weekend that he would like to revise the school history curriculum to include 'the rise of western domination of the world' as the 'big story' of the past 500 years, the Education Secretary, Michael Gove, leapt to his feet to praise Ferguson's 'exciting' ideas – and offer him the job.

Ferguson is a poster-boy for big stories about big empire, his books and broadcasting weaving Boys' Own-style tales about the British charging into the jungle and jolly well sorting out the natives. The *Independent*'s Johann Hari, in his capacity as young bloodhound of the liberal left, sniffed out Ferguson's suspicious narrative of European cultural supremacy in a series of articles in 2006, calling him 'a court historian for the imperial American hard right': Harvard-based Ferguson believes that the success of the British empire should be considered a model for US foreign policy. This is exactly the sort of history that British conservatives think their children should be learning. 'I am a great fan of Ferguson, and he is absolutely right,' Michael Gove told the *Guardian*.

The new Education Secretary has declared his intention to set out a 'traditionalist' curriculum 'celebrating' Britain's achievements. Andrew Roberts, another historian lined up to advise on the new curriculum, has dined with South African white supremacists, defended the Amritsar Massacre and suggested that the Boers murdered in British concentration camps were killed by their own stupidity. It looks like this 'celebratory' curriculum might turn out to be a bunting-and-bigotry party, heavy on the jelly and propaganda.

What should shock about these appointments are not just the suspect opinions of Roberts and Ferguson, but that the Tories have fundamentally misunderstood the entire purpose of history. History, properly taught, should lead young people to question and challenge their cultural inheritance rather than simply 'celebrate' it.

'Studying the empire is important, because it is an international story, but we have to look at it from the perspective of those who were colonised as well as from the British perspective,' said the historian and political biographer Anthony Seldon, who is also Master of Wellington College. 'We live in an interconnected world, and one has to balance learning about British history with learning about other cultures.'

The ways in which schools and governments structure and promote stories about a country's past, the crimes they conceal and the truths they twist, have a lasting effect on young minds. It is not for nothing that the most fearsome dictators of the twentieth century, from Hitler to Chairman Mao, altered their school history curricula as a matter of national urgency.

Even now, the school board of the state of Texas is rewriting the history syllabus to sanitise slavery and sideline figures such as Thomas Jefferson, who called for the separation of church and state. That the Tories, too, wish to return us to a 'traditionalist' model of history teaching should thoroughly disabuse the left of the notion that the present-day Conservative Party has no ideological agenda. The drive to rehabilitate a nostalgic vision of Britain's imperial past is part of the same bigoted discourse in which the new Defence Secretary, Liam Fox, recently described Afghanistan as 'a broken thirteenth-century country'. It appears to be forming Conservative thought at home and abroad.

This week, an ugly caricature of inner-city teenagers appeared on the Tory-affiliated website ConservativeHome. The post, which laments that in Hackney 'the white middle-class people disappear as soon as it gets dark', is titled 'How the East was Lost' – drawing an explicit parallel between the resistance of colonised populations to British military rule and resistance of voters in inner-London areas with large ethnic-minority populations to Conservative ideas. The writer parodies the accents and eating habits of Hackney teenagers with the revolted fascination of a Victorian colonel writing about the natives, implying that these 'fatherless, swaggering, out-of-control' youths need a firm white Tory hand to keep them in line.

Michael Gove's wish to re-engineer how history is taught to children is, quite simply, about social control. It is part of a broader political discourse that seeks, ultimately, to replace the messy, multivalent web of Britain's cultural inheritance with one 'big story' about dominance and hierarchy, of white over black, west over east, rich over poor.

But history is not about the big story, the single story, the story told by the overculture. History is not about 'celebrating' the past, nor about making white kids feel good about their cultural inheritance. History is a process of exploring the legacy of the past, and questioning it – including the ugly, uncomfortable parts. No wonder the Tories want to tear it up and start again.

THE POWER OF THE INTERN

9 April 2011

The internship system is a murky pool of privilege and influence. Over the last week, since the government's social mobility strategy dragged the issue into the news, we have heard a great deal about the advantages of doing an internship in government, media or finance for those lucky youngsters who can afford a shortcut into top jobs. But we have heard rather less about the effect that unpaid interns can have on employers.

The problem is twofold. It's not just the thousands of pounds of free labour that graduates offer, meaning that many worthy liberal organisations now find themselves in the awkward position of financial dependence on a practice that skews the job market in favour of the children of the wealthy. It's also the interns themselves, and the influence they can have on the daily workings of the British political machine.

Interns shape the atmosphere of an office. The director of a think tank, canvassing opinions for his latest report, might ask the young man making coffee what he and his friends think about taxation. A magazine editor, looking for features that tap into the zeitgeist, might ask the girl doing the photocopying what the kids are excited about these days. I should know: I've been an intern. As one of the thousands of posh dogsbodies propping up the liberal establishment, I was often asked what young people were thinking on any given issue, as if I, with my Oxford degree and nice rounded vowels, somehow represented everyone under 35.

The only young people decision-makers now meet on a daily basis come from privileged backgrounds. They are often the sons and daughters of colleagues, who will not be affected, for instance, by cuts to benefits that enable poor teenagers to complete their A-levels. That's not all, however. Lobbying groups can also manipulate the internship system for their own ends. A worrying example is the fundamentalist Christian group dedicated to ending legal abortion in the UK that is giving tens of thousands of pounds worth of interns to MPs.

For several years Christian Action, Research and Education, a lobbying group whose mission is to 'bring Christian insight and experience to matters of public policy', has poured money into providing MPs with free researchers. It spent more than £60,000 in 2008–9 alone, providing eleven MPs with interns when anti-abortion amendments were passing through the Commons. Every one of the Conservative MPs who was provided with a free researcher by Care voted to restrict access to abortion. This year, with fresh anti-abortion proposals being pushed through parliament, four MPs currently have interns sponsored by the Christian group. These interns have Commons passes and access to parliament at the highest levels.

As a charity, Care has a legal duty not to 'give support or funding to a political party, candidate or politician', and inquiries have been made by the Charity Commission and in parliament. No clear decision has yet been made, however, as to the ethical position of lobbying groups who sponsor politicians by proxy, paying interns to pick up their dry cleaning. Care is unlikely to be the only organisation paying to place young people with approved views in influential parliamentary roles.

Of course, the principle of paying for internships was endorsed by the Conservative Party itself. At the party's annual fundraising ball, wealthy donors made bids for coveted placements with City banks and law firms, forking out thousands for their own children to slide painlessly into positions of power. It underlines that the internship system is both unfair and open to abuse by vested interests. Ending unpaid internships would be a good start: but the trail of money and influence runs deep.

STRICTLY COME SCROUNGING?

30 October 2010

Even in hard times, nobody likes a scrounger. As the country trembles under the Tories' fiscal hammer, no-one seems to want to contest the popular political narrative that welfare recipients have had it far too good, and must be punished. George Osborne has declared that his downsizing of the benefit system, which could force hundreds of thousands into abject poverty, will 'incentivise' jobseekers towards employment – because apparently all it takes to solve the problem of millions out of work is a little get-up-and-go. This is social security as reimagined by Simon Cowell – only life's winners are rewarded, and losers go home empty-handed.

The cynical amongst us might contend that 'making work pay' is rather a tasteless euphemism for 'cutting welfare so savagely that even the minimum wage looks like unattainable luxury' – but we live in a rat race, and the sick, the needy and the unemployed have proven themselves insufficiently murine. They are losers, they lack the X factor, and since there's no glamour in compassion, we've just voted them all off the welfare programme.

Labour MPs, who began the bloodless process of privatising the welfare system in 2007, seem to have accepted that the PR battle over 'benefit scrounging scum' is unwinnable. This is because Britain has slowly but surely become a country that does not tolerate failure. The emotional logic of our society is now one of ceaseless neoliberal striving, a tyranny of aspiration.

Failure is a dirty word in modern Britain. Our sudden distaste for bankers' bonuses is not grounded on antipathy for extreme wealth but on simple annoyance that financiers are being rewarded for getting it wrong. The desperate tyranny of aspiration is also the reason that so many of us spend our Saturday nights glued to the *X Factor*, or *The Apprentice*, or *Dragons' Den*: these reality talent shows are compelling collective expressions of the fantasy that anyone can make it if we try hard enough. Life is a competition, and if we fail to please the bosses, their dull orange faces plasticised at great expense into permanent expressions of self-regard, we only have ourselves to blame.

The X-factor vision of society, placing all the blame for failure on the individual, is a seductive narrative. Most of us would far rather believe that the poor are lazy and stupid than countenance the notion that the rich and powerful are steering us gleefully over an economic precipice. It's far easier to blame the poor for not working than it is to blame the system for not working.

Reality television bleeds into political realism at every fissure, and with Alan Sugar now sitting in the Lords, perhaps it would be more honest if the benefits system were simply rearranged according to the formal rules of a TV talent contest. We could call it *Strictly Come Scrounging.* Instead of the current welfare tests, which already force disabled people to touch their toes and walk until they fall over to justify their claims, why not go the whole hog and turn the process into a glitzy musical freakshow? We could choreograph the unemployed into a magical land of jobs with a spring in their step and a song in their hearts. If they're any good, claimants could be required to give open-air performances so that better-off members of the Big Society can finance their penury directly, without tiresome state intervention. We could give it a fancy name, like 'begging'.

As the foundations of social democracy are dismantled before our eyes, ordinary people dream of the transcendence of celebrity. Researchers found that fame is the number one ambition of today's eleven-year-olds, and no wonder – the lottery of stardom must now look slightly more winnable than the scramble for a decent standard of living if you happen, like many TV talent show contestants, to have been born poor.

Perhaps a different approach is in order. If our political settlement is starting to resemble reality television, then maybe the best response is to make the television look more like the kind of political realism we'd like to see. Why not unionise the *X Factor*? Picture the scene: next week, during the finalists' group number, the contestants suddenly stop singing all at once. They turn to the judges and declare that they are now the United Saturday Night Musicians League, and they believe in collective bargaining. A large percentage of the programme's profits are to be immediately redistributed amongst all entrants for their time and labour, or there will be no show. The contestants then proceed to sing the 'Internationale' in memory of their fallen comrades, Diva Fever. Imagine the look on Simon Cowell's pitiless potato face.

POVERTY PIMPS: SELLING OUT THE DISABLED

24 January 2011

Of all the obdurate lies peddled by the Conservative Party in the run-up to the last general election, perhaps the most callous was when the Tory disability spokesperson Mark Harmer told key representatives of Britain's millions of disabled and mentally unwell citizens: 'I don't think disabled people have anything to fear from a Conservative government.' It turns out that disabled people have a great deal to fear.

Despite a fraud rate of just 1 per cent, the government is determined to toss 500,000 people who currently rely on sickness benefits into the open arms of the bleakest labour market in a generation, to cut already meagre disability stipends to starvation levels, to confiscate mobility scooters and community groups from the most needy, and to remove key services that make life bearable for thousands of families with vulnerable relatives. The party assures us that someone's got to pick up the tab for the recklessness of millionaire financiers. So, naturally, they're going to start with the disabled and the mentally ill.

Disabled people, their friends, family members and allies, have much to fear – and much to fight. Today has been designated a national day of action against benefit cuts, and resistance groups across the country will be staging protests and spreading the word about how the government's plans to dismantle most of the welfare state and privatise the rest will affect them. 'Housing benefit cuts mean I'm probably going to lose my home,' says Carole, 32. 'But the removal of the Incapacity Benefit safety net means that I'm terrified of looking for work. If I'm made to do a job I'm not well enough for and have to leave, I'll be left penniless. I don't know what to do.'

Many of the demonstrations will target private companies like Atos Origin, which has been given government tender to impose punitive and – studies have shown – largely unreliable medical testing of welfare claimants before forcing the sick to seek work that even the healthy can't get. Campaigns like Benefit Claimants Fight Back are quite clear what they think about these companies – they are 'poverty pimps'.

As Britain's welfare claimants who are well enough to do so take to the streets, the beleaguered workers responsible for administrating the ersatz and vituperative benefits system have just finished a 48-hour strike over the way their jobs are being restructured to meet increasingly high targets of claimant turnover. 'The system is driven towards saving money at the expense of vulnerable people. We want to help people but they're not letting us,' says William, a 22-year-old worker in a call centre that deals with Incapacity Benefit claims. 'You get old people phoning up in floods of tears when their relatives have died.'

'I hate them calls. We're so limited in what we can say because all our calls are recorded and they watch us all the time. You're chained to your desk. It's hell working here,' he says. 'We have people off sick with stress all the time – I've had to take medication for anxiety and I normally consider myself quite a strong, down-to-earth person,' he adds. 'People come to work in tears, but they're terrified of saying they can't cope, because they know just what happens if they have to go on the sick. Nobody wants to have to deal with our system from the other end.'

The withering of the welfare state is not just a party game. The gradual erosion of the principle, formalised in the Attlee settlement, that people who are unable to work and support themselves should not be left with nothing to live on, did not start with this government. Labour formalised the process in 2008, mounting grandiose campaigns against 'welfare cheats' and flogging off support services to private companies whose express purpose was to deny benefits to as many people as possible – including, in several cases, terminal cancer patients. The argument, put forward by many commentators, that punitive welfare reform can't be that bad because 'Labour started it', is the political equivalent of sticking your fingers in your ears and humming to block out the angry cries of a million human beings deprived of their dignity.

This is more than a party game. For New Labour, the financial intimidation of the sick and vulnerable was, in part, a desperate appeal to the prejudices of voters in marginal seats, a strategy tried and tested by PR professionals in Bill Clinton's second term who later came to work for the Blair/Brown administration. Bullying people off benefits, however, is about more than just votes. It's part of a creeping cultural shift towards a public consensus that there is no room in this society for the weak.

In this country and across the developed world, labour is precarious, competition for jobs and adequate pay is fierce, workers are under terrific pressure and anyone who cannot keep up with the rat race, whether through sickness, mental ill health or physical disability, is mistrusted and shamed. 'My clients frequently express more shame that they are not able to work than over the perceived inferiority of their bodies,' comments an anonymous disability worker. 'In a materialist society, apparently, the ultimate failure of the disabled is that we don't make money.'

We like to think of ourselves as a nation where, if anything, 'political correctness' has gone too far, but our attitude towards people with disabilities and mental health problems has barely improved in 20 years. A recent survey revealed that four out of five employers would prefer not to take on anyone with a history of mental health problems. Meanwhile, rather than question the terms of a target-driven labour market whose precariousness routinely drives workers to the edge of mental and physical breakdown, ordinary people are taught to kick down savagely at any fellow citizen who can't keep up.

This is not just about a culture that puts profit before people. This is about a culture that has begun to believe, on some deep and terrifying stratum, that if one cannot turn a profit, one is not really a person at all. Disabled people and their allies are fighting back in whatever way they can. Shame on the rest of us if we do not fight with them.

A TALE OF THREE PARTIES

27 September 2010

Manchester, 2008. With the financial edifices of Wall Street and the City of London tumbling like dominoes, the Labour Party faithful have gathered at the annual *New Statesman* conference reception to soak away their panic. In the grand, high-ceilinged ballroom of the town hall, the old neoliberal certainties are dissipating like chill vapour: the one question on everyone's lips is whether David Miliband, a man who ideologically and personally resembles the banana-grasping voodoo corpse of Blairism left to rot in a pool of inertia for two years, will make a bid for the leadership and reanimate the only model of electoral success the left has known in the past generation.

Meanwhile, a young cabinet minister with an awkward haircut, who is at this point most famous for not being David Miliband, takes the platform to deliver some calming platitudes. Miliband Minor's soothing quips about the humiliations of being a younger brother fall on dull ears. Everyone is more intent on drinking hard – drinking with the cheery desperation that only the British can muster when the streets are on fire and the bar is free.

Fast forward to Brighton, 2009. In the dying days of the last Labour administration, the great and good of the British left have once more gathered at the *New Statesman* party to drown their sorrows. The recession has hit hard, and nobody now believes that Labour will win the next election; privately, there are many who suspect that it might not deserve to win. The corporate lounge at the soulless seafront hotel gradually fills with bewildered delegates, drifting through the glass doors in ones and twos with the shell-shocked expressions of war refugees. The room is too bright, full of static and suspicion; knots of gossip and weary recrimination cluster in the corners of the party. It's like the disco at the end of the world.

The speaker this year is David Miliband, but unfortunately, just as he is ushered onto the stage, somebody brings out the booze. The party faithful charge across the crackling carpet towards the bar like victims of a natural disaster mobbing a Red Cross van, only with substantially less dignity. Nobody listens to Miliband Major, and why would they? The jaws of the credit crunch are snapping shut, and Torygeddon is approaching: not even Blairism can save us now.

Fast forward to this weekend: it's the 2010 Labour Party conference, and we're back in at the same party, in the same lofty setting as 2008 – the decadent Victorian granite of Manchester Town Hall. And this time, everybody is waiting for Ed Miliband. The shy junior cabinet minister from 2008 has just been anointed leader of the Labour Party in a nail-biting victory over his elder brother, the heir apparent. We have watched his strange rubbery face on the front pages and ubiquitous television screens for 24 hours, and now we are waiting anxiously for Ed like schoolgirls waiting for their prom date to arrive.

When he finally does arrive, flanked by beaming young volunteers who have just been elevated to the status of political flunkies, a spontaneous cheer erupts: a triumphant, rather irreverent cheer, peppered with whoops and wolf-whistles. Ed Miliband is manifestly not the revivified corpse of Blairism – instead, even with the heady flush of new leadership, he still calls to mind the dorky, swotty kid at the back of the class to whom, for some indefinable reason, nobody has paid much attention. Until now.

Ed takes the stage and tells us, with a rather sad smile and not a hint of swagger, that he wants the Labour Party to change. He wants the Labour Party to show humility over its past mistakes, and to 'question old truths'. He wants the Labour Party to be the 'natural home' for the next generation of activists, in part because it is young volunteers who have made his campaign such a success. He wants the party to unite, to abandon factionalism, and most of all – more than anything – he wants 'change'. Unlike the smooth, polished Anglo-American political salesmen of the post-crash era, you suspect that he actually means it.

It is perhaps a testament to how comfortable the Labour Party has become with hierarchy and privilege that the sudden leadership of Ed Miliband – who is, after all, not an outsider, but a son of leafy north London from a distinguished Labour lineage, whose only claim to political insurgency is that he is not the elder brother – should have so shaken the party faithful. In a truly radical party, this would not have been so stunning a change of direction, but New Labour has not been truly radical for many years.

Expectations were low, and this is enough; it's enough to tremble the foundations of the British left and disturb its stagnant, hierarchial customs, so reliant on anointed heirs and settled successions of power. The gathering at the *New Statesman* party is suffused with panicked excitement. The delegates are behaving like a group of normally compliant school pupils in an empty classroom, when someone unexpected – say, the dorky kid at the back of the class – has just got up from his place and sat down in the teacher's chair. It's a scandalous, it's thrilling, it's surely against the rules!

The overwhelming impression is that anything could happen, and the room bubbles with breezy expectation and just a suggestion of naughtiness. Personal and political seductions are attempted; old friendships and alliances are rekindled. Delegates flirt, make eyes at one another and have meaningful discussions about the living wage and progressive taxation over glasses of orange juice, the boozing less frantic than in previous years.

It's been a long hangover, but this morning, the British left is finally knocking back the Alka-Seltzer of humility and stumbling to its feet. After all, there's work to be done.[16]

SIMON HUGHES AND THE CARTEL OF BRITISH POLITICS

2 January 2011

It's January and the sales are on but austerity isn't selling as well as the coalition had hoped – so a new, conciliatory marketing drive has been launched to win fickle customers back to neo-Thatcherism.

As David Cameron, head of PR for UK plc, released a decidedly defensive new year's press statement assuring consumers that the coming cuts to public services are 'not ideological', it was announced that the deputy Liberal Democrat leader Simon Hughes MP is to be the new face of privatised higher education, in much the same way that Natalie Portman is the new face of Dior.

Hughes, who abstained from the vote on the Higher Education Bill and spoke out against measures to triple university fees and slash teaching and research funding, has now been recruited literally to sell these same measures to the betrayed young people of Britain.

16. Unfortunately, one year on, the Labour Party still can't find its ideology with both hands.

'The problem with the system is the perception rather than the reality,' said Hughes, whose new role as 'advocate for access to higher education' will see him trying to persuade poorer teenagers that lifelong debt is no reason not to go to university and join the bargain-bucket scramble for the educational opportunities that their mothers, fathers and political representatives enjoyed for free.

Hughes will be taking his higher education roadshow to deprived schools and under-funded sixth-form colleges over the next six months, a glorified door-to-door salesperson for unpopular Tory policies, an Avon lady for Thatcherite university reform. The dogged, defeated hypocrisy of this former rebel Lib Dem's decision to accept the appointment is far from the most compelling thing about this story.

The truly fascinating aspect of this brazen attempt to win over wavering liberals is what it reveals about the way in which the new right understands its role in office. This is not just government run in the interests of business – this is government run as a business. This is a government perceiving its proper purpose as the sale and promotion of privately run services and small-state moral evangelism to the consumers it once called citizens.

The Conservative Party seems quite seriously to believe that there is nothing untoward about deciding on a policy, keeping it quiet until after election day, forcing it through the Commons in the face of overwhelming public opposition and then recruiting friendly faces to sell it back to the nation in a shiny yellow package. Right-wing ideology has become a simple sales drive and all that is solid, as Mark Fisher observed in *Capitalist Realism*, melts into PR.

During a recent radio debate, I found myself arguing about NHS privatisation with the Cabinet Office minister Oliver

Letwin, who simply could not understand why I would not want my health-care providers to consider me 'a valued customer'. When I responded that I did not want to be treated as a customer but rather as a citizen who deserves the best possible chance at health, he seemed genuinely confused. Unfortunately, treating citizens like customers doesn't always mean that they are more valued – companies, after all, are not ultimately answerable to their customers, especially when those customers happen to have no money.

Telling voters that the only problem with a government decision is our 'perception' of it, rather than the fact that it might be dangerous, reactionary bullshit, is an intricately patronising political long-game. By setting political 'perception' as the province of the people against political 'reality' as the province of those in power, this government has made it quite clear what it thinks of the hoary old notion of parliamentary mandate. If you're unhappy with the products and services provided by UK plc, then one of our helpful advisers will be able to assist you in changing your mind.

When governments are run like companies, democratic choice is subsumed within consumer choice, which is increasingly no choice at all. Instead of real democracy, we now enjoy a limited selection of extremely similar neoliberal schemata sold by two or, at most, three companies. Instead of ideology, we now have 'aspiration' and 'lifestyle choices'. If we shop elsewhere for social justice, we are informed that browsing for politics outside of the big established brands will deliver an inferior product and quite possibly social meltdown. There is a word for this sort of monopoly. The word is cartel.

British politics has become a brutal cartel, offering only the illusion of choice, branding and rebranding itself to reflect rather than represent public feeling. The government is running scared, however, and the decision to change its core message to a defensive one, a message of damage control, offers hope – not empty aspiration but real hope. It offers the hope that, one day soon, we might be able to take this shoddy coalition back to the dodgy counter where it was sold to us under false pretences.

THE SOCIAL MOBILITY SCAM

7 April 2011

If you want to slip an awkward truth past the guard dogs of Middle England, it helps to throw them a bone of contention. Last week, in a bid to set the terms of the new class debate, universities minister David Willetts MP casually mentioned that it might actually all be women's fault. Willetts's words, to the effect that mass female employment has been the 'biggest single factor' holding back working men, were tossed out just in time to cause maximum controversy in the Friday headlines and the Sunday columns. And off we all went, yapping after the bait, the liberal left and the chattering classes, barking and bickering between ourselves.

Have women sold out working men? Have working men sold out women? While the commetariat pondered these questions, everyone failed to draw attention to the solid, foundational fact that it is the rich who have sold out the poor, mortgaging their life chances to pay the debts of global finance.

Over the course of a fortnight, conservative spin-doctors have performed an exquisite feat of repositioning. Framing the initial debate as a whodunnit – which sex killed social mobility? – lays down two important principles as a given. Firstly, that social mobility is the highest possible public good; secondly, that whoever is responsible for the nosedive in social mobility since the 1970s, it definitely wasn't the free market.

Willetts's notion that 'feminism has trumped egalitarianism' holds no water. Ask any unemployed labourer in any of the thousands of northern towns eviscerated by Thatcher's maceration of industry what's really holding them back, and chances are they won't say 'women'. The delusion that women selfishly taking the jobs and university places that should have gone to working-class men, and then even more selfishly refusing to sleep with them – a practice which Willetts delicately calls 'assortive mating' – distracts us from the greater truth that the social mobility experiment of the mid-century is over.

Today, children born to working-class parents are overwhelmingly likely to remain working class. Children who go to low-achieving schools usually end up in low-paying jobs, especially in former industrial towns. Wage repression has meant that it is now nearly impossible to raise a family on a single person's wage, meaning that most couples with children are obliged to work two full-time jobs between them. Labour has become more precarious, and structural unemployment has continued to rise. Top jobs in politics, journalism, law, management, business and finance are held in trust for the sons and daughters of the wealthy, as opportunities go to those who can afford to work as unpaid interns or, increasingly, to pay for vital work experience. In fact, like nearly every other journalist under 35, the main reason I have this platform to talk to you now is that I'm a beneficiary of the private-school-and-intern system.

All of that was the case even before the June 2011 budget. Now, an increase in regressive taxes that hit the poorest hardest, a threefold increase in university fees that places higher education beyond the reach of many, and the withdrawal of the few remaining benefits, such as Education Maintenance Allowance, that really did help young men and young women of all ages to cross class boundaries, have lacerated the ailing proto-corpse of social mobility in Britain. The government's suggestion that sending a few civil servants to give motivational talks in schools will somehow solve the problem is the equivalent of smearing a little ointment on a gushing arterial neck-wound.

The cuts are already too fast, and too deep: the body politic is bleeding out. The government has begun to panic, desperate to stem the flow of public opinion in the best way it knows how: by appealing to the self-interest of the sharp-elbowed middle classes. Middle England cares about social mobility. Middle England wants its sons and daughters to be wealthy. Unfortunately, its sons and daughters are currently sliding onto the graduate scrapheap, stuck on the dole or in dead-end jobs, or tearing through the streets of London in masks and hoods, smashing up banks. This is not good news for coalition approval ratings.

If the Tories are to retain power, public discourse has to be shifted, and it has to be shifted fast. Nobody who has so much as squinted at growth projections could claim that social mobility is likely to do anything but decline in this country for the foreseeable future, but that's not what matters to the government. What matters is the appearance of concern, a shadow-play of interest in helping the 'squeezed middle' – a catch-all term for electorally crucial swing voters – rise through the ranks.

A brief shuffle through the social mobility strategy turns up glossy pages of utter vacuity, full of platitudes, vague half-policies, disclaimers explaining that government can't do all or indeed really any of the work, and doleful insistence that 'there is no magic wand we can wave'.

Perhaps the most interesting part of the document, however, is the opening premise: 'a fair society is ... a society in which everyone is free to flourish and rise'. Social mobility is apparently this government's 'principal' social concern. But are fairness and social mobility truly synonymous?

Social mobility, lest we forget, is not the same thing as equality. On the contrary: the entire premise of social mobility rests on the blithe acceptance of social inequality, so long as a handful of have-nots are able to scale the ladder of privilege. In a world where wealth and resources are finite, not everyone can be a billionaire. The encouraging notion that anyone can 'make it' relies on the unspoken assumption that most people, ultimately, won't.

That vision of unfettered self-improvement is the lie that has sustained free-market capitalism over a century of ruthless expansion. It is the lie that neoliberal governments across the developed world have used to justify the destruction of welfare, healthcare and education, the decimation of labour and the entrenchment of inequality along divisions of race, class and gender. It's a lie that convinces most when it is most manifestly false: indeed, recent studies have shown that in America, the more social mobility decreases, the more desperate voters are to believe that 'anyone can make it if they try'. It is the cross-continental American Dream, the dream of enterprise as redemption, the dream that, in the words of the late George Carlin, 'you have to be asleep to believe'.

Let's return to David Willetts, whose opening salvo makes the bigoted assumptions behind our understanding of 'social mobility' plain. There are a finite number of places 'at the top', for which citizens of all classes are supposed to compete. Middle- and upper-middle-class men have first dibs on those places, and after that, middle-class women and working-class men are allowed to slug it out for the scraps. Working-class women rarely get a look-in, but that's social mobility for you.

Social mobility is a scam. It's a scam that is useful to governments implementing austerity programmes: after all, if anyone can make it, anyone who fails to do so must be personally at fault. Social mobility, however, is not an adequate substitute for social justice. Which brings us neatly back to feminism, and to the uncomfortable admission that David Willetts does, in fact, have a point. Mass female employment has affected social mobility. Feminism is nowhere near as significant a factor in the stagnation of social mobility as the destruction of industry or wage repression. The fact remains, however, that if one accepts an unequal system whereby only a handful of elites make it into well-paying professions, and if one also accepts a feminism which settles for cramming a few extra women into those elite jobs, then some people are going to be nudged off the podium. What we have, to paraphrase Willetts, is neither feminism nor egalitarianism. What we have is a ruddy mess of recrimination and sharpened elbows.

Willetts has a point, and he is using that point to stab innocent bystanders in the back. Along with most of Westminster, Willetts has mistaken bourgeois feminism, which merely boosts the life chances of wealthy women within an unequal system, for feminism proper, which demands redistribution of work, wealth and power in order to deliver equality. Along with most of the country, Willetts has mistaken social mobility, which merely boosts the life chances of a few middle-class aspirants, for social justice. As inequality soars and the standard of living in Britain drops through the floor, those mistakes are about to cost us all very dearly.

IV
Cultural Capital

'The function of art is to renew our perception.
What we are familiar with we cease to see.'

Anaïs Nin

FACEBOOK, CAPITALISM AND GEEK ENTITLEMENT

1 October 2010

The Machiavellian machinations of modern capitalism become a lot clearer when one realises that much of it is built, owned and run by people who couldn't get a girlfriend in college. *The Social Network*, David Fincher's film about the founding of Facebook, is an elegant psychodrama of contemporary economics: flash, fast-moving and entirely founded on the principle of treating other human beings as hostile objects.

The film's basic formula is the familiar blogs-to-bling-and-bitches redemptive parable of male geek culture, with the added bonus that it happens to be based on real events. The protagonist, Facebook's co-founder Mark Zuckerberg, is a brilliant 19-year-old coder. His painful social ineptitude, as told here, gets him savagely dumped by his girlfriend, after which, drunk and misunderstood, he sets up a website to rate the physical attractiveness of the women undergraduates of Harvard, thus exacting his revenge upon the female sex that has so cruelly spurned his obvious genius.

We know by now, however, that unappreciated nerds eventually grow up to inherit or at least aggressively reappropriate the earth, and so it is for Zuckerberg: his website becomes the prototype for Facebook, a venture that will eventually make him a billionaire, mobbed by beautiful groupies and hounded by lawsuits from former friends and business associates desperate for a share of his fame and fortune. It's a fairy-tale happy ending, as imagined by Ayn Rand.

The Social Network is an expertly crafted and exhaustively modern film, and one of its more pertinent flashpoints is the reminder that a resource that redefined the human interactions of 500 million people across the globe was germinated in an act of vengeful misogyny. Woman-hating is the background noise of this story. Aaron Sorkin's dazzlingly scripted showdown between awkward, ambitious young men desperate for wealth and respect phrases women and girls as glorified sexual extras, lovely assistants in the grand trick whose reveal is the future of human business and communication.

The only roles for women in this drama are dancing naked on tables at exclusive fraternity clubs, inspiring men to genius by spurning their carnal advances and giving appreciative blowjobs in bathroom stalls. This is no reflection on the personal moral compass of Sorkin, who is no misogynist, but who understands that in rarefied American circles of power and privilege, women are still stage-hands, and objectification is hard currency.

The territory of this modern parable is precisely objectification: not just of women, but of all consumers. In what the film's promoters describe as a 'definitively American' story of entrepreneurship, Zuckerberg becomes rich because, as a social outsider, he can see the value in reappropriating the social as something that can be monetised. This is what Facebook is about, and ultimately what capitalist realism is about: life as reducible to one giant hot-or-not contest, with adverts.

There is a certain type of nerd entitlement that is all too easily co-opted into a modern mythology of ruthless capitalist exploitation, in which the acquisition of wealth and status at all costs is phrased as a cheeky way of getting one's own back on those kids who were mean to you at school. As somebody whose only schoolfriends were my Dungeons & Dragons team, I understand all too well how every socialist and egalitarian principle can pale into insignificance compared to the overwhelming urge to show that unattainable girl or boy who spurned your dorky sixth-form advances just what they were missing.

The narrative whereby the nerdy loner makes a sack of cash and gets all the hot pussy he can handle is becoming a fundamental part of free-market folklore. It crops up in films from *Transformers* to *Scott Pilgrim vs. the World*; it's the story of Bill Gates, of Steve Jobs, and now of Mark Zuckerberg. It's a story about power and about how alienation and obsessive persistence are rewarded with social, sexual and financial power.

The protagonist is invariably white and rich and always male – Hollywood cannot countenance female nerds, other than as minor characters who transform into pliant sexbots as soon as they remove their glasses – but these privileges are as naught compared to the injustice life has served him by making him shy, spotty and interested in *Star Trek*. He has been wronged, and he has every right to use his l33t skills to bend the engine of humanity to his purpose.

This logic is painful to me, as an out-and-proud nerd. For a person with a comics collection, an in-depth knowledge of the niceties of online fan fiction and a tendency to social awkwardness, it is distressing to see geekdom being annexed by the mythology of neoliberal self-actualisation. There's far more to being a geek than maladaptive strategies that objectify other human beings as hostile obstacles who deserve to be used to serve the purpose of one's own ambition, but watching *The Social Network*, you wouldn't know it. For me, being a geek is about community, energy and celebration of difference – but in the sterile fairy tale of contemporary capitalism, successful geekery is about the rewards of power and the usefulness of commodifying other humans as a sum of likes, interests and saleable personal data.

The tragedy of *The Social Network* is also the intimate tragedy of an age whose self-alienation has nothing to do with social networking. The paranoid atomisation of modern social relations has, in fact, very little to do with the internet at all. It has everything to do with a global economic machine that trains human beings to understand one another as manipulable objects or faceless consumers. That, unfortunately, is a trend that did not start on Facebook.

GIRLS, TATTOOS AND MEN WHO HATE WOMEN

5 September 2010

For a long time, I refused to read Stieg Larsson's *Millennium* trilogy.[17] Not out of disdain for popular fiction, nor because of the many objections in feminist circles to the books' graphic depictions of sexual violence, but because I judge books by their covers. I simply declined to spend my money on one more novel entitled *The Girl With the Distinguishing Physical Attribute of Minor Narrative Significance*.[18]

Having been thoroughly bored by *Girl With a Pearl Earring* and *The Girl With Glass Feet*, I naturally assumed that *The Girl With the Dragon Tattoo* would be stuffed with

17. *The Girl with the Dragon Tattoo, The Girl who Played with Fire* and *The Girl who Kicked the Hornets' Nest*, Quercus, 2008, 2009, 2010.

18. Also out of personal trepidation. It has been pointed out to me several times that I resemble Larsson's description of Lisbeth Salander, being very short, pouty, pale, dark and a bit of a goth, with a predilection for hoodies and murderous personal revenge.

monotonous, sexist clichés. So, imagine my surprise when I discovered that not only is the *Millennium* franchise a global pulp fantasy crammed with dashing heroines taking bloody and unorthodox revenge on male abusers, but the original Swedish title of the first book is *Men Who Hate Women*. The English-language publishers found this sentiment rather too confrontational, and it's not hard to see why.

I now can't help grinning every time I see prim ladies in office suits reading the *Millennium* books on public transport, or scrutinising the posters for the hugely popular film adaptations, the second of which is currently in UK cinemas. Larsson, who died of a heart attack just before the trilogy was published, was disgusted by sexual violence, having witnessed the gang rape of a young girl when he was 15. According to a friend of his, the author never forgave himself for failing to help the girl, whose name was Lisbeth – just like the young heroine of the trilogy, who is also a rape survivor.

Lisbeth Salander is an immensely powerful character, a misandrist vigilante with a penchant for black fetish wear and ersatz technology, like the terrifying offspring of Batman and Valerie Solanas. She is so well drawn that one can almost forgive Larsson for having her sleep with the protagonist (an obvious author-insert of the kind normally only found in teenage fan-fiction) for no discernible reason. Salander is smart, she's brave, she always wins, and she won't let anyone tell her what to do. No wonder so many women secretly want to be her.

It is clear that the author of the *Millennium* franchise did not intend to glamorise violence against women. Unfortunately, it's rather hard to stop the heart racing when rapes and murders are taking place in gorgeous high-definition over a slick soundtrack: part of the purpose of thrillers, after all, is to thrill. Decorating a punchy pseudo-feminist revenge fantasy in the gaudy packaging of crime drama rather muddles Larsson's message. 'Misogynist violence is appalling', the series seems to whisper. 'Now here's some more.'

However, the real problem with sensationalising misogyny is that misogyny is not sensational. Real misogyny happens every day. The fabric of modern life is sodden with sexism, crusted with a debris of institutional discrimination that looks, from a distance, like part of the pattern. The real world is full of 'men who hate women', and most of them are neither psychotic Mob bosses nor corrupt business tycoons with their own private punishment dungeons under the putting green. Most men who hate women express their hatred subtly, unthinkingly. They talk over the heads of their female colleagues. They make sexual comments about women in the street. They expect their wives and girlfriends to take responsibility for housework and to give up their career when their children are born.

Most rapists, similarly, are not murderous career sadists who live in flat-pack Ikea torture palaces conveniently rammed with incriminating recording devices. Most rapists are ordinary men who believe that they are entitled, when drunk, angry or horny, to take violent advantage of women who know and trust them.

Equally, most men who see women as objects don't dismember them and stuff them into rucksacks. They visit strip clubs. They watch degrading pornography. If they work, just for instance, in publishing, they might reject a book title that draws attention to violence against women and replace it with one that infantilises the female protagonist and focuses on a trivial feature of her appearance.

Cathartic though revenge fantasies may be, not every woman is a ninja computer hacker with street fighting skills, and fantasies that divide men into sadistic rapists and nice guys obscure the subtle matrix of real-world misogyny. Real misogyny requires a sustained and subtle response. And real sexism, unfortunately, can't always be solved with the judicious application of a Taser and a tattoo gun.

PICKLING DISSENT

24 March 2011

The modern resistance movement has been cannibalised by capital with astonishing speed – from bank campaigns urging potential customers to 'join the revolution, to *Vice* magazine's decision to stage an 'edgy' fashion shoot in the middle of the December riots. Now Jake and Dinos Chapman, those erstwhile 'bad boys' of British art most famous for making huge plastic children with penises where their noses should be, have decided to drum up some publicity by sponsoring the student protesters.

Genuine dissent attracts artists and hustlers like a suppurating wound attracts flies. The Chapmans, along with Damien Hirst and other no-longer-quite-so-young members of the Young British Artist school, have created a fund to pay the fines of prosecuted student protesters in order to, in Jake Chapman's words, 'mock the government'. Other wealthy professional rebels, from Clash legend Mick Jones and Primal Scream's Bobby Gillespie to top designer Stella McCartney, have also pledged their support in this month's *Dazed and Confused*. Student protesters have so far declined this high-profile offer of assistance.

Young British artists like the Chapmans and Tracey Emin – now a noted Conservative supporter – made their millions with 'edgy', 'ironic' art designed to give liberal sensibilities a naughty thrill. There is nothing edgy or ironic, however, about the anti-cuts movement, which is far bigger than just students. The efforts of affluent pseudo-agitators to vampirise and appropriate the only honest-to-God counter-culture this country has seen for a generation is deeply offensive to those who are preparing to put their jobs and bodies on the line to fight the government's austerity programme.

The half a million mothers, trade unionists, benefit claimants, office workers and children who will march this Saturday will not be doing so to make trouble for fun and profit. We will march because we cannot do without healthcare, welfare, decent wages, public services and education. We will march because we have no choice but to march.

Real resistance is many things, but it is not cool. Cool is what happens when capital appropriates the counter-culture – a sanitised dissent that can be mass-produced and printed on cheap T-shirts.

It is significant that the celebrity pledge-bank has declined to offer its support to any of the less fashionable branches of the protest movement: single mothers, disabled people, public-sector workers and the mentally ill are clearly not cool enough for the Chapmans, nor for any of the advertisers and fashion flunkies who have tried to capitalise on the energy of the student protests. Their struggle, however, is equally urgent.

The age of ironic art is over, because the age of irony is over. Ordinary people have begun to articulate an alternative to the desperate nihilistic glut of the 1990s, and George Osborne's plan to fund the banking crisis by tearing the heart out of the welfare state has stirred the sleeping monster of popular dissent. The ironic shrug, the desire to shock people momentarily in between coffee and the gift shop, is no longer an adequate response to political expediency. What is required is resistance, and real resistance cannot be rehabilitated. The slogan of the modern resistance movement is a clarion cry against irony and apathy, scrawled over occupied classrooms and the wall of the Treasury: 'This is actually happening.'

Drawing 'edgy' art and ironic fashion out of a serious ongoing social movement is grisly social taxidermy, an attempt to turn the awakened beast of public defiance into – in effect – a pickled shark in a tank. A pickled shark in a tank is shocking, but it is safe. The real, open-eyed rage of ordinary people is never safe. It is, however, actually happening.

JULIE BURCHILL'S IMPERIALIST RANT OVER ISRAEL

13 February 2011

In this week's column, shoved in underneath some musings about comedy and refried beans, the *Independent* rentagob Julie Burchill takes a detour into the sort of stuttering imperialist froth that Russell Brand might refer to as the Bad Zionism.

Burchill denounces the latest popular explorations of Israeli politics – Channel 4's drama *The Promise* and Louis Theroux's documentary exposé of ultra-Zionist lifestyles in Jerusalem and the West Bank – as foaming anti-Semitism, borne out of Gentile resentment that Jewish people are good at science.

No, really. Burchill really does argue that discussing the most fraught, difficult and painful topic in modern international relations in any terms that do not automatically grant the Jewish people every disputed square mile of moral high ground, because they 'built the country we call Israel centuries before Islam even existed', is just bitchy bitterness about so many 'Jews winning the Nobel Prize'.

Yes, it's bonkers, but there's bile behind it. Burchill stubbornly fails to draw any distinction between the blithely racist, imperialist ultra-Zionists in Theroux's documentary and the more reflective and compassionate politics of the vast majority of Jewish people. In fact, most Jews feel about as much kinship with ultra-Zionists as most Christians feel with the more fundamentalist members of the Westboro Baptist Church. In Burchill's eyes, though, it's all just 'Jew-baiting'. Showing Israeli soldiers firing tear gas canisters at Palestinian children in Hebron is 'Jew-baiting'. Dramatising the agonising conflict between Jewish war refugees searching for a home and Palestinian families being violently evicted from their land is 'Jew-baiting' and nothing more.

I know it's not about me, but as a woman of Jewish descent with many family members living in Israel, I find this sort of reductive bollocks personally offensive. In point of fact, *The Promise* is not a piece of propaganda. Rather, it is a reflective and excruciatingly well-researched series that throws light on a segment of British wartime history that most Brits prefer to ignore – namely, our own involvement in the creation of the state of Israel and our complicity in the decades of bloody conflict that followed.

It's hard to understand how anyone can accuse a drama that opens with five gruelling minutes set in Bergen-Belsen concentration camp, cutting in segments of real footage from the mass graves, of ignoring the tragic nuances of Jewish history. For Burchill, though, since the series stops short of declaring all Palestinians criminal trespassers, it's just more 'Jew-baiting'.

For some people, history is just a creative space for redrawing the bloody map of the moral high ground to suit your own dogma. For others, history drives right up to your front door on a daily basis in armoured tanks, penning your family behind gun-bristling checkpoints, cramming your friends and neighbours behind an 'apartheid wall', bombing your home, machine-gunning your grandchildren.

Dragging all discussion of the suffering of the Palestinian people back to a dry debate over whose tribal deity promised them the land most flamboyantly is a wilfully clod-headed rehearsal of what George Orwell called transferred nationalism – 'power-hunger tempered by self-deception'. Ultimately, if we're really going to play the who-got-here-first game, someone really needs to put in a word for the poor old Philistines. And the Caananites. And the Midianites. And the Amalekites. And the followers of Ba'al, all of whom have some prior historical claim on the land by virtue of being slaughtered or enslaved or driven out over the course of three millennia of gory religious tribal wars – it's all there in the Torah. The sort of self-deception that calls all temperate inquiry 'Jew-baiting' is just dogged, ahistorical worship of the politics of bullying.

BABY BOOMERS

26 July 2010

If there is one thing that sets the baby boomers apart, it is their dogged rejection of history. For those born between 1945 and 1955, the past was peopled with timid, elderly, authoritarian figures whose ideology had no place in the new world order. This reckless refusal to locate themselves in the long march of human social development is perhaps what led Francis Fukuyama, one of the baby boomers (he was born in 1952), to mistake the end of the cold war for the 'end of history'.

Fukuyama was wrong: history never ends, and in refusing to remember the hard lessons of the early twentieth century, the members of the postwar generation may, in Francis Beckett's assessment, be 'fated to force [their] children to relive it'. His book[19] adds a welcome dose of perspective to the popular mythology of this unusual generation, setting the baby boomers in context and dissecting their shortcomings.

'The world they made for their children to live in,' Beckett writes, 'is a far harsher one than the world they inherited.' He argues that the radicalism of the 1960s and 1970s was made possible by the Attlee settlement, which blessed the baby boomers with affordable health care, decent housing, free higher education and a generous welfare state that liberated them from immediate cares – all blessings that they declined to pass on to the next generation. 'It is as though the Sixties generation decided that the freedom from worry which they had enjoyed was too good for their children,' Beckett says.

There is no mercy in the book for this generation – the generation of my parents – which 'squandered the good times' on childish pseudo-radicalism that 'was all done by smoke and mirrors', and which demanded respect while it was young before obliging its overextended offspring to foot the bill for its unthinking excesses.

Beckett acknowledges that his book does not offer an 'objective history of the Sixties'. Instead, he selects events

19. Francis Beckett, *What Did the Baby Boomers Ever Do for Us?*, Biteback, 2010.

and quotations that bear out his unflinching thesis. At times, the selection can feel uneven: for example, he returns repeatedly to the addictions, aphorisms and assorted other personal failings of the young Marianne Faithfull, but devotes less than a paragraph to the defeat of the striking miners in 1984–5. His argument is most powerful when he ties the lives of big-name individuals such as Gordon Brown and Tony Blair to the social psychology of 17 million Britons.

Peppered with vignettes from the lives of Blair and Brown, as well as extended interviews with other influential boomers such as Greg Dyke and Peter Hitchens, the book is, in effect, a lyrical biography of the Sixties generation. It patiently explains how each successive decade formed its collective personality, with particular focus on the vicissitudes of the British left. There are several moments of dizzying cultural and historical vertigo as Beckett charts the transformation of Brown, Jack Straw and Charles Clarke, among others, from edgy, arrogant student defenders of the grants system into the 'grey, pompous, reactionary' senior politicians who presided over the dismantling of free higher education.

What Did the Baby Boomers Ever Do for Us? offers no easy solutions, and is less a call to arms than a self-flagellation manual for middle-aged sell-outs. This is entirely appropriate; as Beckett rightly observes, the country is owned and run by those same middle-aged sell-outs, and many of them could do with a little flagellation. After all, they've had it their own way for rather more than six decades.

It could be argued that Beckett is excessively unforgiving in portraying the hypocrisies of the boomer generation. And it should certainly be remembered that while it seems all of Beckett's friends have sold out, there are many boomers who did not. Many retained their idealism, refused to throw their lot in with neoliberalism, and still see the social and cultural transformations of the 1960s as current. Consider, for instance, the partial victory of the women's movement and the huge gains made for homosexuals and people from ethnic minorities, none of which gets more than a cursory mention in Beckett's proudly unbalanced survey. We could, in short, be generous.

But why would we want to do a thing like that? Why do the baby boomers deserve a generous and forgiving assessment, having failed to show a shred of comparable generosity to the generations that followed them? *What Did the Baby Boomers Ever Do for Us?* returns Sixties mythology to history. And if the picture is warped, it is so for good reason: the mirror Beckett holds up to the recent past is smeared with the suffering of young people today.

BAH, HUMBUG

20 December 2009

Something about this Christmas sticks in the craw. It's not just the creeping sense of frustrated greed, more bitter this year because of the extra hundreds of thousands out of work – it's the fact that we're all supposed to be so cheery about it, gleefully swapping our usual extravagances for home baking, knitting and making natty little baubles out of bits of string and glitter.

Newspapers are full of editorials urging their female readers to 'have a crafty Christmas' by hand-making gifts and decorations. These articles are inevitably accompanied by soft-focus photos of terrifyingly blonde, grinning women in shapeless knitwear fashioning entire kitchen sets out of balsa wood, like a cross between a nuclear strike advice handbook and the Boden catalogue.

This bizarre fashion for retro handicrafts started some years before the credit crunch with the revival of Stitch 'n' Bitch knitting circles in New York. This was initially conceived as a fun, feminist reclamation of traditional skills: the meetings were free, the skill-sharing amiable. But as the recession has taken hold, the trend has been co-opted by the dark machinery of the women's lifestyle press, desperate for a new manifesto to replace 'shop 'til you drop'.

Despite the impact of the recession on women, who are losing their jobs faster than men in the financial, leisure and hospitality information industries and facing redundancy and discrimination at work because of pregnancy or motherhood, there's an atmosphere of celebration. According to the *Evening Standard* and many, many others, we're all becoming 'domestic goddesses' again. Don't fret about losing your job – for the price of a shedload of specialist ingredients you too can bake sparkly fairy cakes, stave off economic Armageddon and save Christmas.

The most brain-bleedingly pointless domestic tasks are now thoroughly fetishised – as long as it's women acting out that fetish, of course. Cookery classes and exclusive sewing circles encourage young, trendy women to indulge in a sanctioned fantasy of glamorous drudgery that never really existed. For just £310 a session, 'recessionistas' can have a training day with Cookie Girl in Notting Hill. Sales of kitchen equipment are rising faster than an organic souffle.

Now, no-one's implying that a little more domestic dexterity wouldn't do all of us some good. Certainly, decades of aggressive marketing of home improvement products, the revolt against traditional gendered labour divisions and the male backlash against that revolt have led many to abandon the basic tools of self-care. What is being lost is not a prim model of Beetonesque housewifery, but the essential human tricks of keeping ourselves clean, clothed and fed.

The current craze for sexed-up retro-domesticity does nothing to remedy this. Instead of everyone rediscovering truly useful, empowering self-care skills, women alone are being encouraged to spend vast sums on instruction and materials for pastimes that have almost no bearing on their actual lives – pastimes that are performative rather than practical. Who, when you get down to it, really needs to know how to knit a Christmas fairy or ice a lavender cupcake à la Nigella Lawson?

Of all the fluffily sexist trends to come out of 'post-feminism', this one truly unnerves me. I know women my age and younger, educated and emancipated, who have no idea how to make a stock or take in a hem but view the baking of immaculate muffins and the embroidering of intricate scarves and mittens as exciting hobbies, pastimes which should be properly performed in high-waisted fifties skirts and silly little pinafores. Wouldn't it be great, the subtext runs, if we could just go back to the way things were then – when women were real women, men were real shits and the mince pies were really scrummy?

Of course none of this fantasy, performative retro domesticity has any basis in reality. Such hedonistic time wastage has all the historical accuracy of the sort of sexual role play which involves Victorian schoolboy outfits and birch whipping canes. Like all such fetish play it is perfectly jolly fun as long as it isn't taken seriously. But if unexamined, there is always the risk that a fetish will bleed into reality.

I refuse to be a 'recessionista.' I will not have a Crafty Christmas, thanks. I will not be spending my afternoons this

December making elegant hat-pieces out of potato peelings or fashioning festive cake decorations from cat litter, or in any way fantasising about being a suburban housewife in a haze of Valium in some ad-man's wet dream of early post-industrial capitalism. Not now, not ever.

But what do I know? Stockists of craft supplies, baking equipment and ridiculous frilly aprons have all seen a jump in profits and in even jollier festive news Associated British Foods is reporting a 35 per cent increase in sales of bun trays. Let choirs of angels sing.

INTERVIEW WITH CHINA MIÉVILLE

21 September 2010

China Miéville is rather suspicious of stories for someone who makes a living writing them. 'I'd advocate a certain amount of scepticism towards the healing power of storytelling or the emancipatory potential of narrative,' he says. 'I think a lot of it is essentially winsome propaganda put out by writers trying to aggrandise what they do.'

Having won a host of prestigious fiction awards – most recently for his arcane thriller *The City and the City*, which received the Hugo and Arthur C. Clarke awards in 2010 – Miéville perhaps has no need to self-aggrandise. His latest book, *Kraken*, has been enthusiastically received within and outside the traditional science-fiction fanbase, and it is refreshing to hear a writer who makes a living breaking the rules of genre and structure call the monolithic mythology of the power of stories into question.

'In our world, narrative is inevitable,' says Miéville. 'It's also what pays my mortgage, so if I thought it was inevitably toxic I like to think I wouldn't engage.

'Storytelling is clearly an extremely important function of societies, but it's nonetheless unproven that to be human is to be a storytelling being. Even if it is the case that human beings are completely intrinsically storytelling animals, it doesn't follow that that's something to celebrate, any more than we should celebrate the fact that human beings are defecating animals.'

Miéville really does speak like this – in quiet, precise received pronunciation, like an excitable, brilliant sixth-former with a dictionary, a scatterdash instinct to self-justify and a powerful desire to shock. At well over six feet tall with huge shoulders, a boxer's figure, a shaved head and a gleaming array of silver earrings cast from octopus tentacles, Miéville is an intimidating presence, less like a stereotypically retiring SF writer than an otherworldly force of nature, strangely ageless at 37.

Stalking through his creepily opulent north London living room, which is stuffed with comics, drawings and strange talismanic ornaments in glass cases, he cuts the sort of figure who might be more at home on the decks in a rave club or brooding on the doors of a Soho occult society than appearing on Radio 4's *Front Row*, where he is due this afternoon, as one of the rising intellectual stars of his generation.

Miéville is, in short, nauseatingly cool – but the speed at which he rattles through ideas rather prevents you from holding it against him.

'As readers and thinkers, we may want to celebrate some aspects of storytelling, and we may find some of it dangerous,' he says. 'Even if you say the human mind is addicted to storytelling – well, humans get addicted to all sorts of things that aren't good for them.'

'That perspective is important for socialists, too,' explains Miéville, who is a committed Marxist and a prominent member of the Socialist Workers Party. 'Stories can be a useful way of exploring politics, but it really depends on what you're trying to do.

'If you're political, then politics is an inevitable part of everything. On the other hand, I do think politics is particularly pointed in science fiction, because science fiction is predicated on alterity, and alterity is an intrinsically political concept.

'Science fiction and fantasy are always predicated on the idea that the impossible is true, that the not-real is real, and that's surely an idea that has a lot of political ramifications. How can it not?'

Miéville himself has been political 'since I was about 12 – I was involved in issue politics, in youth CND and the Anti-Apartheid Movement, stuff like that, and then when I went to university I was doing a lot of reading and meeting people with strong erudite opinions, and auditioning various paradigms in my head.

'It's very easy to roll your eyes about young people getting passionately into political ideas, but that's how I moved away from left postmodernism and into a search for political totality, into Marxism and socialism.'

Alongside his many literary accomplishments, Miéville holds a PhD in international relations from the London School of Economics, is on the advisory board of the Marxist journal *Historical Materialism* and is co-editor of the anthology *Red Planets: Marxism And Science Fiction*.[20]

'That stuff is in my fiction because I'm interested in it, and because having characters struggle with racism, sexism and

20. Pluto Press, 2009.

labour disputes brings, paradoxically, an element of realism to the unreal. On the other hand, I don't feel restricted to the fantastic as political ventriloquism – stories can't be reducible to a leaden allegory or they won't work.

'If I want to write something that's about the war in Iraq, I'll write something about the war in Iraq. I'm not living in the Soviet bloc in the 1980s, nobody's stopping me from doing that.'

Miéville's socialist politics break through everywhere in his novels, which have cut a niche for themselves by self-consciously locating scenes of social struggle and workers' uprisings within the tropes of fantasy and weird fiction. 'Representations of revolutionary change can be particularly fraught and difficult for writers who are actually committed to it,' he explains. 'If you tell a story about a people's revolution, and you depict it failing, then you're essentially slipping into that tragedian paradigm whereby even if it's desirable it can't ever really happen.

'On the other hand, if you show revolution succeeding, I think intrinsically and inevitably you end up banalising it. In my novel *Iron Council*, I tried to take seriously that dilemma and show the notion of revolutionary potential not as failed, and not as frozen, but as imminent in the everyday, all the time.'

Miéville has just launched into a serious discussion of the effects of consumerism on culture when the doorbell rings. He bounds down the stairs like a man possessed – an accessory for his new iPad has just been delivered.

'What're you going to do, consumerism, well, you've got to buy stuff to live,' he explains rather sheepishly, fondling the surprisingly enormous cardboard box. 'And sometimes when that stuff is just so lovely ... you have to surrender, I suppose.'

I ask if he and the box would like to be alone together for a while. Miéville seems to consider the proposition for an agonising split second, before deciding that the politics of storytelling are just too important. He pours tea from a silver teapot and calms down a little.

'You can't escape narrative, and as a culture we need to think so much harder about how stories are deployed politically,' he explains. 'Narratives can be very powerful without convincing anybody.

'For example – very few serious thinkers believed there were weapons of mass destruction in Iraq. Very few people on the street thought there were weapons of mass destruction in Iraq. But that's the story that made the running, and homogenised that whole area of discourse. So those of us who are opposed were running around shouting: "No, there aren't any weapons of mass destruction" – but maybe we should have been saying something more like, "fuck this absurd agenda! I'm not going to argue on this ludicrous axis, this isn't what war is about!"

'There's a real political importance to questioning the power of stories, and it's something that, as radicals, we definitely shouldn't trivialise.'

I SHALL WEAR MIDNIGHT

28 October 2010

Tiffany Aching, the teenage witch who stars in Terry Pratchett's latest novel *I Shall Wear Midnight*,[21] is in many ways the anti-Harry Potter.

21. Terry Pratchett, *I Shall Wear Midnight*, Doubleday Childrens, 2010.

True, she's a precocious pubescent who gets to ride a broomstick and save the day, but the final installment of her four-novel series of adventures is no jolly tale of boarding school, wand-waving and chocolate frogs. In fact, it is highly likely that a book so savagely bleak as *I Shall Wear Midnight* has not been marketed to children since the days of Struwwelpeter.

For example, not 30 pages in, Tiffany is called to assist when a pregnant 13-year-old miscarries after being assaulted by her violent, alcoholic father. The young witch is able to use hedge-magic to take away the girl's pain before burying the foetus; the father later hangs himself. Hogwarts, it ain't.

Scenes like this are tempered by a grim, melancholy maturity. When we first met her in *The Wee Free Men*, Tiffany was a gutsy nine-year old; now aged 15, she is a fully-fledged local witch and an important figure in the local community. Her exhaustive responsibilities involve everything from nursing dying pensioners to delivering babies, most of which she does thanklessly, in the face of well-drawn rustic misogyny.

Pratchett seems to suggest, with his characteristic gentle humour, that this is what growing up is like: full of hard work, disappointment and death. When one understands that the author himself is in the grip of a debilitating degenerative illness that has already robbed him of his ability to type, and is a prominent campaigner for the right to euthanasia, the brooding, serious atmosphere of *I Shall Wear Midnight* begins to make sense.

This is not in any respect a silly book. Yes, fairies are involved, but the Nac Mac Feegle largely steal sheep and start bar-fights, like some of the more frightening wee folk of ancient legend. Pratchett is an incisive folklorist, and the Tiffany Aching series comes doused in a cold shower of British country arcana, of the sort that tends towards vigorous knob gags and nature red – or at least suspiciously brown – in tooth and claw. There is no room on the Discworld for wilting maidens in high turrets or the gooey pan-Celtic romanticism that oozes through much modern pulp fantasy.

Indeed, a recurring theme of Terry Pratchett's young adult fantasy is the special disdain he reserves for blushing princesses and silky-haired young ladies in silly frocks. In Pratchett's oeuvre, beautiful airheads who mope around waiting for their prince to come are at best a waste of space, at worst dangerously inept: inevitably, they have to be rescued and re-educated by sensible brunettes a fetish for old books.

This perennial Pratchett double-act is played to great effect here, pitting Tiffany in a restrained battle for the bumbling young hero against a simpering proto-princess named, fittingly, Letitia. As a mousy, bespectacled teenager, one of my favourite things about Pratchett's books was his instinctual understanding of the unfairness of fairy tales that mandate, as the worldly protagonist of *I Shall Wear Midnight* observes, that 'only blonde and blue-eyed girls can get the prince and wear the glittering crown'. As an adolescent, I found Pratchett's relentless disapprobation of pretty, popular girls rather satisfying, but as an adult, the trope is slightly more problematic; one learns that in many cases, young ladies with highlights and impractical shoes also have souls.

Nonetheless, Tiffany is the sort of heroine I wish had been able to read about when I was 15. She's a gutsy, sensible farm girl with ambition and the instinctive, unselfish heroism of wise children. She's a terrible broomstick-rider, and her sidekicks include a toad and an anthropomorphic cheese. She commandeers the help of powerful, wonderfully rounded older women characters to fight the forces of bigotry and misogyny – for what else, in the language of fairy tale and allegory, is witch-finding all about?

Tiffany Aching would not be happy at Hogwarts. For her, being the witch is about 'not having to be stuck in the story'. Faced with a world of brutal superstition, she sets out to change it, teeth gritted, broomstick in hand. At the close of this remorseless folk tale, though, is a moment of redemption: growing up may be difficult, even in a fairy tale, but with Terry Pratchett, there's always at least the possibility of a happy ending.

IT'S ALL OVER FOR SEX-AND-SHOPPING FEMINISM

27 May 2010

Girl power is over. The release of the second *Sex and the City* film, in which four rich Americans analyse their marriages on a boringly opulent girls' holiday to Abu Dhabi, sounds the death knell for a pernicious strain of bourgeois sex-and-shopping feminism that should have been buried long ago at the crossroads of women's liberation with a spiked Manolo heel through its shrivelled heart.

Any woman who claims not to enjoy *Sex and the City* is still considered to be either abnormal or fibbing, at least by a certain strain of highly paid fashion columnist whose lives probably bear an unusual resemblance to that of the show's protagonist, the lifestyle writer Carrie Bradshaw. For the young women of my generation, however, *Sex and the City*'s vision of individual female empowerment rings increasingly hollow, predicated as it is on conspicuous consumption, the possession of a rail-thin Caucasian body type, and the kind of oblivious largesse that employs faceless immigrant women as servants.

What young women want and need today is secure gainful employment, the right to equal work, the right to make decisions about our bodies and sex lives without moral intimidation, and the right to be treated as full human beings even if we are not beautiful, skinny, white and wealthy.

Much ink has been spilled over whether the swinging sexual empowerment epitomised by *Sex and the City*'s insatiable Samantha Jones is a positive erotic model for women, or whether Samantha's orgasmic adventures, squealingly portrayed by Kim Cattrall, are simply obscene. In fact, the real obscenity of Samantha's lifestyle has nothing to do with her bedroom antics.

In the first film, a minor plot-hook hinges on the character's fancy for an antique ring costing $60,000, which is eventually, to her chagrin, bought for her by her boyfriend. The type of feminism that gives serious thought to whether a girl should buy her own diamonds has missed something fundamental about the lives and problems of ordinary women.

Like any glamorous fantasy, *Sex and the City*-style feminism is only harmless when it does not haemorrhage into reality. Unfortunately, female empowerment under Britain's new centre-right coalition government also seems to be more about the shoes than the substance. Gushing attention has been paid to the extensive footwear collection of the new Home Secretary and Minister for Women, Theresa May, by press outlets all too keen to minimise her appalling record on gay rights and her punishingly pro-life agenda.

With May and her fellow female cabinet member Baroness Warsi dubbed the coalition's 'fashion double act', it seems as if all it takes to be pro-woman today is a really killer pair of heels. But May and Warsi are doing nothing to stop the coalition, as one of its first acts in power, from proposing what amounts to a rapists' charter.

Just this week, the new government found time in its recession-busting schedule to table a law that offers anonymity to men accused of rape, who are considered special victims of what the *Mail* calls 'extreme man-hating feminism'. No similar anonymity is being extended to those falsely accused of child abuse: women are being singled out as liars by a government that appears to support rape culture.

Meanwhile, in the real New York City, millions of women are living in poverty without adequate housing or health care, and an underground abortion railroad assists other American women denied essential reproductive services. And in Abu Dhabi, the 'glamorous, exotic' setting for the faux-feminist narrative of *Sex and the City 2*, rape victims are jailed, and husbands are allowed to beat their wives with sticks.

Fortunately, today's young women, growing up post-recession, are less susceptible than the previous generation to having our heads turned by fashion, fortune and the weary phallic cipher of Mr Big. *Reclaiming the F Word* by Catherine Redfern and Kristin Aune[22] charts the emergence of a new breed of feminist: young, political, pragmatic and attuned to issues of class and race, violence and power that are elided by sex-and-shopping feminism.

A fantasy feminism of shopping, shoes and shagging is not an adequate response to a world that still fears women's power and punishes our bodies. 'If pop culture's portrayal of womankind were to be believed, contemporary female achievement would culminate in the ownership of expensive handbags, a vibrator, a job, a flat and a man,' comments

22. Zed Books, 2010.

the feminist academic Nina Power, whose book *One-Dimensional Woman*[23] advocates a more radical basis for feminist thought than whether one is willing to spend $500 on a pair of Jimmy Choos.

Hadley Freeman of the *Guardian* confirms that the second film heralds the death of the *Sex and the City* franchise. Good. It needed to die. It was a pernicious, elitist meme that distracted us from the real problems facing women's liberation in the twenty-first century. In a world where rape accusation is still considered a more serious crime than rape, the feminists of the twenty-first century want more from life than marriage, babies and a really great shoe collection. We want power, fairness and freedom from fear, and we're coming to claim it. Girl power is over: long live the new feminism.

BEYOND NOUGHTIE GIRLS

2 August 2009

I'm facing a feminist dilemma. A few weeks ago, I agreed to review a book written by a friend and ally of mine, a woman I deeply respect. *The Noughtie Girl's Guide to Feminism*, by Ellie Levenson,[24] is an attempt to merge the type of froth-feminism peddled by *Cosmopolitan* and *Glamour* into something more meaningful and coherent. It's a flouncily inoffensive go-to guide for the type of modern woman who likes the idea of self-respect and empowerment but is frightened that feminist politics comes with a mandatory

23. Zero Books, 2009.
24. Ellie Levenson, *The Noughtie Girl's Guide to Feminism*, Oneworld, 2009.

buzz-cut, all wrapped up in a kitsch pink cover with the ubiquitous pair of disembodied stilettoed legs that screams, 'whatever this is it's disguised as chick-lit!' Unfortunately, the disguise works a little too well.

Which is where my dilemma begins. I agree that feminism needs to reach out to the mainstream, to women who wouldn't normally think of themselves as feminists, but still enjoy the rights feminism has won for them. I applaud the fact that more feminist books are being written with today's young women in mind. I'm definitely over the moon that one of my feminist mentors has finally managed to secure a publishing deal and expand the remit of websites like The F-Word which have kept the coals of feminist movement glowing in these dim post-backlash times. But I can't get around it: *The Noughtie Girl's Guide to Feminism* makes me angry. It makes me want to throw things at walls. It makes me want to actually set fire to my actual bra whilst I'm still wearing it and run flaming through the streets of Hackney yelling 'How did we come to this?'

Petty arson aside, the real heartbreak of *Noughtie Girls* is that both the concept and execution are so very spot on. I adore the fluffy, frilly presentation, the demotic language, the stubborn refusal to get bogged down in high theory, which has its place, but not in an introductory book for sceptical feminists. I love the way the whole thing is structured in bitesize crossheads, making it easy to open at any page and find something interesting. I even like the silly little *Cosmo*-esque 'what kind of feminist are you?' quiz at the front of the book, which shaves gleefully close to self-parody. It's perfect Tube-reading. It's fun. It's accessible. It's the sort of thing that I might give my little sister for Christmas, sandwiched between something smelly from The Body Shop. But here's the rub: it apologises too damn much.

The book comes across as an apology for a brand of 'man-bashing, bra-burning' feminism that never really existed. It spends altogether too much time dismantling the straw woman of the feminist who would forbid pretty young ladies from waxing their legs and wearing pink, and altogether too little time explaining why it is that that sort of feminist only exists in the nightmare fantasy Britain conjured up by editors at the *Daily Mail*. It spends so much time debunking the myth, telling its readers that it's OK to be a 'Noughtie Girl' who likes high heels and pink drinks, that it ends up reinforcing the idea that 'traditional' feminism is something to fight against.

Secondly, for a primer, *Noughtie Girls* is very limited in scope. It is rigidly heteronormative in its approach – and this is a deliberate strategy – because as Levenson notes in her warm-up: 'As I have no direct experience of many of the issues specifically concerning lesbians I have not attempted to cover these here.'

It also fails to take into account the special problems that women can face if they are disabled, living on a lower income, or from a black or minority ethnic background. Of course, feminism applies just as much to prim middle-class women who have never kissed a girl or liked it – but equally, a part of feminist experience has to be about challenging received norms of gender, culture and sexuality, including our own. The experiences of lesbian and bisexual women, to take just one example, cannot be erased from a primer on feminism without presenting a flawed picture of what feminism really is. It's not a question of lack of experience: it's a question of simple lack of research, or, more worryingly, lack of interest in the relevance of feminism to women who are not white, straight and middle class. *Noughtie Girls* is right to address itself to the common woman – but by ignoring swathes of the female population, it makes a great deal of common women invisible in the process.

The third thing that makes me uncomfortable with *Noughtie Girls* is its defeatism. It is a book which self-assuredly talks about 'choice' and 'equality', whilst happily accepting that we're always going to live in a world riddled by gender inequality and rent by social rules that ruin the lives of both sexes. As Levenson says in her recent *Guardian* article:[25]

> Perhaps the key difference between me and my critics is that while I am keen to look at our everyday lives in the context of the society in which we live, they seem to prefer the idea of overthrowing the patriarchy – the belief that society is run by men to the detriment of women. Not only do I think it is impossible to start again – redrawing society from the beginning according to an equal opportunities policy – but if it's just going to be replaced with a prescriptive matriarchy that discounts the idea of individual choice, I am not sure that I want to.

Feminism is not, and never has been, about putting in place 'a prescriptive matriarchy that discounts the idea of individual choice', and Levenson's rhetoric reinforces rather than debunks that tired myth. But more importantly, Levenson has entirely misunderstood what is meant by 'patriarchy'. Patriarchy is not a society 'run by men to the detriment of women'. Patriarchy is a society run by patriarchs – generally older, rich, almost exclusively white people who are almost always men – to the detriment of absolutely everyone else. Fighting patriarchy is not the same as fighting men: in fact,

25. 'Barbie can be a feminist, too', *Guardian*, 30 July 2009.

men have just as much reason to oppose patriarchy as women. Feminists believe that overthrowing patriarchy is achievable, at least in part, because it will involve the emancipation of all citizens from social and gender norms, and every tiny act of self-liberation we achieve hurts patriarchy where it is powerful. This basic misunderstanding warps the premise of Levenson's entire book, and does a disservice to generations of pioneering feminists, including her own.

What *The Noughtie Girl's Guide to Feminism* undoubtedly is, is a classic text of Reformist feminism, a feminist subgroup populated almost exclusively by white, middle-class women like Levenson and like myself. Feminist educator bell hooks explains the term in her excellent primer *Feminism is for Everybody* as follows:

> From its earliest inception feminist movement was polarised. Reformist thinkers chose to emphasis gender equality. [They wanted to] simply alter the existing system so that women would have more rights ... They could break free of male domination in the workforce and at home and be more self-determining in their lifestyles. While sexism did not end, they could maximise their freedom within the existing system. And they could count on there being a lower class of exploited subordinated women to do the dirty work they were refusing to do.[26]

For Reformist feminists, 'choice' is, indeed, the most important remaining feminist issue. But for everybody else, it is a vital aspect in a much wider fight. Opposing patriarchy does not have to be about vetoing anyone's choices, although it may from time to time involve a sisterly criticism of those

26. *Feminism is for Everybody: Passionate Politics*, South End Press, 2000.

choices. It is in a spirit of sisterly constructive criticism, rather than the in-fighting of which Ellie Levenson is so wary, that I was determined to make this review an honest one, rather than offering a disingenuous panegyric or chickening out and handing it to someone else.

Because in one respect, Levenson is right: in-fighting can damage feminism, if in-fighting is all we do. But a homogenous feminist movement without dissent or auto-critique is an even more frightening idea. True feminist sisterhood does not involve not judging other women or other feminists – when it comes to the bedrock ideals of feminism, we can judge, and we should. True feminist sisterhood must also involve debate. It needs to involve exactly the sort of visceral, awe-inspiring energy in debate, in fact, that Levenson's book has instigated on this site and elsewhere. Which brings me on to the biggest sticking point of the entire book: its assertion that 'feminism should not be scary'.

Noughtie Girls is all about making feminism unthreatening, about persuading vacillating women and men that 'feminism is not an ogre', reassuring readers that feminism is really a very gentle movement, all about whose turn it is to do the washing up, full of women who are happy to take their husband's surnames if that is their feminist free choice. But *Noughtie Girls* is wrong. Because, you see, feminism is scary, and it is threatening.

I am not a Reformist. The kind of feminism that I aspire to, along with hundreds of young men and women I have had the privilege to know, is about challenging the identities and roles we've been handed at their very core, even if that means having to re-examine everything about the world we live in. The kind of feminism I see reanimated on the internet and elsewhere does not accept a gender-stratified society, but tries to change and challenge that society one scrap at a time. The kind of feminism I want to help rebuild is, in fact, an ogre, or rather an ogress: colossal, magnificently imperfect and terrifying, with great powerful claws to tear away at the roots of social inequality and unhappiness. I believe that kind of feminism is possible because, in the words of Kathleen Hanna of the punk band Bikini Kill, 'I believe with my whole-heartmindbody that girls constitute a revolutionary soul force that can, and will, change the world for real.'

As Levenson so rightly points out, we can change the world in high heels whilst baking designer cupcakes if that's what we really want. All we need to do is carry on believing that the world can change.

V
Their Hallucinations, Our Desires: The Grassroots

'The only people for me are the mad ones, the ones who are mad to live, mad to talk, mad to be saved, desirous of everything at the same time, the ones who never yawn or say a commonplace thing, but burn, burn, burn, like fabulous yellow roman candles exploding like spiders across the stars.'

Jack Kerouac, *On The Road*

'Destroy their hallucinations with our desires.'

Unauthoured viral poster, London 2011

INSURRECTION ON OXFORD STREET

27 October 2010

'Hey, I want my money back!'

The young man in the grey sweater came to Oxford Street to buy a mobile phone; he isn't part of the gang of activists who have just occupied Vodafone's flagship store. The protesters are in their early twenties, and equipped with banners and placards demanding that the mobile phone company pay the £6 billion in tax that the government allegedly waived earlier in the year, despite the Chancellor's insistence that £7 billion-worth of cuts to welfare benefits are 'necessary'.

This young man isn't part of the group, but he flings himself behind the official cordon, yelling and waving to his friends, who all laugh and get out their mobile phones to take pictures of him. It's a little bit like a Vodafone advert, apart from all the police.

The first thing to note about this protest is that it has been organised only slightly more efficiently than a French farce: the young people currently squatting determinedly in the doorway of the Vodafone store were mobilised via Facebook and Twitter with real names and the intended target freely discussed, and by the time more experienced activists had intervened to give basic security advice, it was too late.

It is, as such, hardly surprising to see Her Majesty's finest waiting for us on Oxford Street, but in the mad dash to dodge the police and barricade the shopfront before the first customers arrive, the protesters giggle like children shocked by their own daring. This is not just the usual troublemakers making the usual nuisance of themselves. They are very young, they are very resolute and they are certain that the left's usual response just won't cut it anymore.

'The next five years can't just be about marching on Whitehall to hear Tony Benn speak,' says Thom, 22. 'We need to get creative.'

The second interesting aspect to this stunt is that it is not an occupation of a government building, or council offices, or a press lobby. Vodafone have had no direct influence over the spending review that will shortly force millions of people out of work and out of their homes and communities. Vodafone do not write Treasury policy. Vodafone sell phones. The people who have gathered to protest here, however, seem to want to articulate a more profound dissatisfaction with the way the new government has decided to prioritise business at the expense of education welfare and healthcare. The public rhetoric of the state emphasises 'fairness' above all else, but those in power seem to believe that fairness is only acceptable if it does not interfere with competition.

'The cuts are not fair, we're not all in this together and there are alternatives,' said another activist, Jennifer Kyte. 'Why not start by collecting – instead of writing off and ignoring – the tens of billions owed in taxes by wealthy corporations? Isn't this supposed to be the wonderful Big Society?'

Nobody attacking the Vodafone store really expects the company to suddenly hand back £6 billion to the state. The matter is settled, after all: Vodafone paid £1.25 billion 'to settle all outstanding CFC issues from 2001 to date and has also reached agreement that no further UK CFC tax liabilities will arise in the near future under current legislation'. Still less does anyone expect that the coalition, which seems to have determined in the coldest reflex of disaster capitalism to use the occasion of the recession to destroy welfare once and for all, will agree to use the money to make sure the poor don't starve this winter. They just want the government and big business to know that unlike Alan Johnson, they can count. They can count, and they don't like the numbers.

All of this feels just a little bit more thrilling than the average rainy protest. Even harried commuters stop to see what's going on. 'I – am – speechless!' enunciates a woman in a smart pink coat. 'What, I pay my taxes but they don't have to because they're a big company?' She fiddles with the police cordon. 'I'm not saying everyone on benefits should be, OK, but I have a friend with five kids, her youngest is eight months, and they've just taken away her benefits, and now you're telling me they let Vodafone off six billion? How's she going to look after her baby now?'

Suddenly, there are screams from the shop entrance. The security doors are coming down and police have shoved themselves into the shop and started dragging out as many people as they can, by their feet if necessary, 'for their own safety'. A girl in a green jumper is pushed roughly to the floor and the rainswept pavement writhes with forcibly twisted limbs as one young man struggles out of the melee and hollers 'Police brutality on the streets of London!' for the benefit of the horrified crowd. We can see what's going on perfectly well.

We can see the police jostling students to the ground. We can see knees going into backs, arms around necks. The small area in front of the Vodafone store has been cordoned off with two violent bandages of red-and-white police tape, and now the agents of the state have surged in to cauterise the wound. Some protesters are now trapped inside; some are linking arms outside the rows of police that now seal off the storefront like a matt black scab. The energy spills out onto the pavement. Like the company they have targeted, these young people are clearly determined to Make The Most Of Now.

With the activists waving a small sea of identical placards with the Vodafone logo and the legend 'tax dodgers', a circle of onlookers get out their phones and start taking pictures. You half expect to hear a smooth voice actor announcing price plans over the cheesy strains of the latest indie-pop sensation, but real life is wetter and angrier than the adverts. All you can hear is the wail of distant sirens.

THIS IS NO CONSPIRACY

26 February 2011

The greatest conspiracies happen in plain sight. Today, across the Northern Hemisphere, activists from the grassroots movement UK Uncut and its newly-formed sister group US Uncut are staging more than 90 protests in local branches of NatWest, Bank of America and the Royal Bank of Scotland, in locations from Hawaii to the English town of Ashby de la Zouch.

The blackboard-happy, shoutyporn shock jock Glenn Beck has denounced this growing movement as a 'conspiracy', telling Fox News that 'this unrest could spread from Middle East to Europe and eventually America ... this would be co-ordinated all around the world'.

Welcome as Beck's condemnation is to left-wing protesters, the yammering wingnut happens to be right. This is indeed a global insurrection, albeit a gentle one, running on poster paint, caffeine and cross-continental co-ordination via horizontal networks and it does come with an overtone of threat. I have spent the past week with members of UK Uncut and affiliated movements as they made placards and managed their Twitter feeds, responding to messages of solidarity from across the world, from Wisconsin to Tahrir Square.

This morning, preparing for the latest protest and slurping down a hasty mug of tea, I watched one activist adjust her leotard for a heroes-and-villains-themed flashmob, accessorised with a cloak bought for a Harry Potter costume party. Her friend, dressed as a tweedy university professor, put on a sinister Death Eater mask. 'Look!' he said, 'I'm Milton Friedman!' Red Army faction, it ain't; but right-wing pundits like Beck are still wetting themselves.

As I write, from one end of Oxford Street in London where 150 Uncutters are marching in the rain, activists are turning bank branches into temporary homeless shelters, libraries and classrooms. These are all vital public services due to be confiscated as world governments impose austerity programmes on their populations in order to bankroll the recklessness of global financiers. The protesters' message is simple: 'The government', in the words of one 42-year-old UK Uncut protester, 'should be making the banks pay, not ordinary people.'

They make their point with flashmobs, bail-ins, street parties for pensioners and pre-schoolers, reclaiming the private space of banks and tax-avoiding businesses, relentlessly restating the hypocrisy of the financial elites. Courageous, yes; Baader-Meinhof-style conspiracy, no. What is most amusing, having spent time with the principled young people who began it all, is how thoroughly the commentariat is failing to understand what the hell is going on here.

The Uncut movement could be kids playing – except that they have a scrupulous economic alternative and an informed network that stretches across the globe. They could be Glenn

Beck's bug-eyed domestic extremists, except that the protests involve toddlers, grannies and young parents with brightly painted placards. In the UK, the police have responded with the classic pose of state agents on the back foot: panicked, malicious bewilderment. A protester shows me photo evidence on her phone of a previous demonstration, when a young woman was dragged away by the police for putting leaflets under a door. 'They used CS spray, and three people ended up in hospital,' she tells me.

Despite the cries of extremism, the Uncut movement is grounded on the same principles of fairness and accountability that politicians have mouthed for decades at the ballot box. Commentators and cabinet ministers nonetheless seem to be shocked by the notion that their electorates can, in fact, count.

Take the UK, for example, where the Royal Bank of Scotland was bailed out with £45 billion of public money – over half the government's £81 billion austerity package – and yet continues to award itself astronomical bonuses. Ordinary people who dare to stand against this manifest injustice are now 'extremists'. Students who post leaflets about tax avoidance through shop doors are 'extremists'. What kind of world are we living in, where wanting local libraries and schools to stay open is now 'extremism', worthy of police crackdowns? What kind of society is this, if it is 'extremist' for people to want to lead decent lives?

Conspiracy-touting like Beck's often looks like plain old scaremongering. In fact, those who toss out conspiracy theories often do so to distract themselves from larger, scarier, less manipulable outrages happening in plain sight. It is easy to rant at anyone who will listen about how the Pentagon bombed the twin towers; it's harder fully to conceptualise that Nato has bombed ten types of bloody hell out of the Gulf for a decade on the slightest of pretexts. Similarly, it is convenient for Beck and other wet-lipped neocon hate-peddlers to claim that the free world is under attack from a network of rabid communist conspirators; it is far less convenient for them to consider the notion that a real people's movement might be on the rise.

The notion that ordinary workers, students, pensioners and parents might finally have found the tools and the impetus to call out the lies of the powerful and demand accountability is deeply uncomfortable for reactionaries everywhere. That notion, the notion of a networked, principled people's resistance, is far more frightening to neoliberal governments than any terrorist cell.

THE REVOLUTION WILL BE CIVILISED

26 August 2010

It's very easy to make fun of hippies. It's so easy, in fact, that the press has largely elided the serious political project that has driven roughly 700 activists to gather outside the Royal Bank of Scotland's Edinburgh headquarters for Climate Camp. Unfortunately, hippies rarely make their critics' jobs harder. Early on a dazzling morning at the makeshift campsite, I am roused from my tent by what sounds like Pink Floyd's apocalyptic children's choir, grown up and grown tone-deaf.

The Climate Campers, most of whom seem to be puppy-eyed graduates in their mid-twenties, are rehearsing a version of Lady Gaga's 'Poker Face' with the words agonisingly rewritten to detail RBS's role in financing the fossil-fuel industry. There are even hand actions.

From the outside, this week-long occupation looks suspiciously like a bunch of students harmlessly pratting about in a field – but through the trees, we can see police in riot vans assembling. What are they afraid of? In the daily consciousness-raising workshops, it becomes clear that the ideology of Climate Camp is impressively nuanced and uncompromising.

'You can't just stand around and shout: 'The system is fucked,' says Sam, a shy 20-year-old who peers at the world from underneath a floppy fringe. 'That's not politics, that's the absence of politics. We need to keep re-examining the interactions of money and power that brought us to this situation.'

Climate Camp is ostensibly as much about anti-capitalism as environmentalism; RBS, which has bankrolled fossil-fuel extraction and is now under public ownership, is being targeted to raise awareness of the links between the two. However, some of the younger campers, having come of age during the worst recession in living memory, feel that the narrative around climate change needs to be more revolutionary.

'Most governments and big businesses have now accepted that we need to tackle climate change,' explains Sam, as we share a filthy roll-up and a surprisingly delicious plate of vegan mess. 'For them, though, that's just about protecting private property. We have to get the message across that climate change is caused by capitalism – and you can't fix one without fixing the other.' Some of the protest stunts border on silly – marching a papier-mâché pig full of oil through central Edinburgh, for instance – but the daily life of Climate Camp is just as important as the direct action.

With gruesomely wholesome reclaimed toilets and chores distributed between all comers, this is more than a campsite – it's a model community built on sustainability and a lack of hierarchy, and the campers are extremely serious about the praxis of the place. 'I'm not just here to protest,' says Annabel, a special-needs teacher working on site security. 'I'm here to up-skill in tools I can use for life in a world without oil and hegemony.'

These are kids who have grown up with structured after-school clubs, summer camps and activity goals – and they are now applying that ethos of managed attainment to their own microcosmic utopia. They may have dreadlocks and may be wearing flowers in their hair but these are not the shambling activists of the 1960s. Everyone is sober and in bed by midnight, and there's no room for mucking about – we've got to be up in time to save the world.

The next day, after mobilising their legal observers and arriving at a democratic action consensus via an arcane process of wiggly hand signals, the campers don biohazard suits and march to RBS headquarters for the first stunt of the day. Expressions of grim commitment belie the cheery carnival atmosphere. Like a genteel, fusty Anglican congregation, the Climate Campers would probably prefer a cup of tea and an awkward sing-song to fire and brimstone any day of the week – but should the necessity arise, they are quite prepared to lay everything on the line for what they believe.

These serious young people did not grow up in the carefree 1960s: they know what a criminal record could do to their job prospects in today's treacherous economic climate. Nonetheless, they storm the bridge, pushing the police out of the way. At the time of writing, at least 12 people have been arrested – and, according to legal observers, two have been hospitalised following alleged police brutality.

This is the future of youth activism in Britain: decked out in silly costumes and socialist ideals, intelligent, iconoclastic and willing to take on the system no matter the cost. As the Climate Campers approach, police are mustering outside the glittering glass of the RBS headquarters. Perhaps they are right to be nervous.

REVOLTS DON'T HAVE TO BE TWEETED

15 February 2011

An extraordinary thing has happened. In Egypt, a million-strong movement forced the overthrow of Hosni Mubarak's government, even though the state had pulled the plug on the internet. After over a week without reliable access to their Facebook profiles, the people of Egypt did not abandon their revolution. They have forced concessions from the government and sent shock waves through the region – without firm help from Twitter. What on earth is going on?

Despite what you might hear on the news, there's a lot more to the recent uprisings than just the knock-on effects of social media. As the world's press has struggled to retain control of the narrative, it has seized on how many of the dissidents are – gasp – organising online. In what appears to be dogged unwillingness to recognise the economic brutality of governments as the root cause of popular unrest, news people everywhere have boggled exhaustively over the way in which protesters in Cairo, Tunis, Paris and London are using the internet to communicate. What did they think we were going to use – smoke signals?

Of course, technology has been a shaping force in these uprisings. The internet is a fascinating and useful tool, the best we have for organising and sharing information. The low cost of participation in digital networks allows protesters to circumvent the sometimes arthritic hierarchies of the old far left and to organise horizontally, while the instant dissemination of camera and video footage and reportage from citizen journalists means that the truth can travel around the world before government propaganda gets its boots on. This has allowed the protests to grow and evolve faster than anyone expected.

At times of crisis, human beings have a reassuring tendency to use the best tools at their disposal to steal a march on the enemy, especially if native fluency with those tools gives us an edge over our oppressors. In these circumstances, it is hardly surprising that young protesters and their allies are organising on Twitter and Facebook.

The internet is a useful tool, but it is just a tool. HTML does not cause mass uprisings any more than a handgun causes mass murder – although, for people of a certain mindset, the mere proximity of the tool is enough to set dangerous thoughts in motion. The internet isn't the reason people are getting desperate and it isn't the reason things are kicking off. Things are kicking off for one reason and one reason alone: there is a global crisis of capital. The writing is on the wall, with or without the web. Across the world, ordinary people – including a huge, seething pool of surplus graduates without employment – are finding their lives measurably less tolerable than they had anticipated. They are realising that they are not suffering alone, or by accident, but because the capitalist classes have consistently put their own interests first.

The writing is on the wall, and it would still be there if we had to paint it on with mud and sticks. Technology is defining the parameters of global protest in 2011 but it is a crisis of capital that has set the wheels of revolt in motion.

IS THAT A TRUNCHEON IN YOUR POCKET?

15 May 2010

So there I am at the gates of Downing Street, at around 3pm this afternoon, with a moderately raucous throng of people in purple demanding 'Fair Votes Now'. We're here to hand in a petition as thick as a man's thigh, demanding a referendum on proportional representation.

And it's all got a bit noisy and spontaneous, in a shufflingly British sort of way, and I've managed to end up at the front of the line, just behind all the people with the huge cameras, who are always there at protests in London but don't really count. This is the closest I've ever been to Number Ten and, aha, here come the vans. Three riot vans screech up and police in yellow jackets pour out of the hatches like predatory lymphocytes to sterilise the dissent. They stream into formation and edge us back from the gates, politely for now, but extremely firmly. One young policeperson's face is really close to mine as he shuffles us unseeingly back, and suddenly, hey! I bloody know you, officer!

Last time I saw Officer X, he was wearing my underwear and a red velvet corset. This was about three years ago, at a photoshoot for a Genet studio show we were both involved in, in which I played a cross-dressing lesbian hooker in eighteenth-century Paris and he played, funnily enough, a career sadist. We were all set up in an empty wine bar to do the shoot for the publicity posters, and we decided it'd look great and also be kinda hot if we swapped clothes.

So we did, and then we did the play, and then we left university and went our separate ways in the way that young people do; me to urban squalor, activism and writing, him to be a state t-cell. I recognised him instantly, because he was doing the same flinty, murderous, slightly suggestive gaze into the middle distance that made his character so effective. He's clearly not going to be on the beat for long.

So I say, 'hey'. And he says nothing. And I say, 'hey', name. And he says, 'oh-er, hi!' His flak jacket is still all up in my face. We exchange awkward pleasantries. Because he's a copper now, he asks me if there really are another thousand of us coming. Because I'm an activist, I deny any knowledge of anything.

The crowd shifts, surges forward behind me, a shifting sea of quiet human rage. We're losing each other in the swell. The moment of connection is gone, and time rushes back with the noise of the chanting and more vans turning up. We promise to contact each other on Facebook, and I disappear into the crowd.

ONE MAN AND HIS TENT

25 May 2010

I'm actually in tears. Boris Johnson, the Tories in Westminster Council and the centre-right coalition have managed to do what nine years of new Labour anti-civil-liberties wrangling didn't have the guts to do. They've sent in the police and they've taken away Brian Haw.

Brian Haw's anti-war protest – a tent, some placards and a whole lot of brazen peacenik courage – has been pitched directly outside the Houses of Parliament for almost nine years. Embarrassing the executive. Reminding them of their complicity in an illegal war. Reminding the people of the possibility of resistance. Labour tried everything they could think of to get rid of him, dragging him through the courts, even setting up a whole new law to ban protest in parliament square without prior approval specifically designed to oust him. They never could. Under the new centre-right regime, however, there's no such faffing about with legal precedent and squabbling over human rights. Today, the Mayor ordered the stormtroopers in to handcuff Brian Haw and drag him away, and now, after nine years, he's gone.

That's what the right does, in government. No lengthy, drawn-out hypocritical bollocks about decorum and protest, no legislating you out of existence bit by heartbreaking bit. Just this. You are a nasty protestor. We do not like you, or your messy ideas about justice and freedom. You are spoiling our nice clean lawn. We are sending large men to remove you.

I am 23, and have been politically active for about as long as Brian Haw's protest has been standing. Nearly all of my significant political memories involve Haw, from rainy pickets over the HFE bill in 2008, to cheering as the crowd of nearly two million marched past his tents on the big anti-war demo in 2003, back when I was 16 and had only just begun to realise how terribly wrong the world was, and the power of personal resistance.

Years later, as a parliamentary intern, I passed Haw's protest every morning and evening as I crossed the street into the Houses of Parliament. And every time, I felt glad to see it, sometimes a lonely one-tent display facing down the glowering edifice of Big Ben and the Commons, sometimes a larger gathering, as thousands of well-wishers and supporters travelled from all over the world to meet Brian and join his demonstration. It made me feel proud, every day, to know that whatever faff was going down in parliament, I still lived in a country where citizens had some right to protest, some right to face down the entitlement and warmongering of the state without fear of their lives and livelihoods, even if it was just one little tent and some placards against centuries of privilege and pride. It made me feel proud, every day. Johnson is using the excuse that Haw's protest detracted from the majesty of Parliament Square, but I considered Brian Haw as much a symbol of the political inheritance of my generation as the Commons. And now he's gone.

Some of us on the left were always convinced that the Tories would be worse than Labour on civil liberties. We did say. But today 'I told you so' tastes of nothing but bile. This is a tragedy, a travesty, and nothing more. Mr Haw, we salute you. The state may want to forget your protest and the grassroots resistance it symbolised. We never will.[27]

HOW THE DISABLED WERE DEHUMANISED

16 December 2010

It's official: disabled people aren't allowed to be independent. This week, amid rows about how this country treats people with disabilities, it was announced that the government will be phasing out the Independent Living Fund (ILF), a vital

27. Brian Haw died of lung cancer in June 2010. He is survived by his seven children and a generation of campaigners who were inspired by his courage.

stipend that allows more than 21,000 'severely disabled people to pay for help so they can live independently'. Such provisions, unlike bank bailouts and subsidies to arms dealers and millionaire tax-dodgers, are no longer a priority for this administration.

When I heard the news, I couldn't help but think of Jody McIntyre, a 20-year-old activist and journalist with cerebral palsy, who I saw batoned and dragged from his wheelchair at the demonstrations last Thursday, and who later delivered a series of epic discursive smackdowns to a senior BBC correspondent on prime-time television.

The press has been trying to imply that, because Jody is a revolutionary activist and ideologue who has travelled to Palestine and South America, he cannot be a 'real' disabled person – he must, as Ben Brown suggested on the BBC, have somehow been 'provocative'. He must have deserved the beating and the humiliation of being pulled out of his chair and across the road; he must have asked for it.

Richard Littlejohn went so far as to compare McIntyre to Andy, a hilariously fraudulent and fatuous wheelchair-using character in the most disgusting pageant of blackface and grotesquerie ever to defile British television screens, *Little Britain*. Like Brown and others, Littlejohn seemed to imply that because he fought back and spoke up, because he attended a protest and because he is not afraid to make his voice heard, Jody McIntyre is not a real disabled person.

Others, including McIntyre himself, have written eloquently about how surprised we really shouldn't be that the police attacked a disabled protester, nearly killed another protester, and injured and traumatised hundreds more. That we live in a state where police officers attack women, minorities and the visibly vulnerable in what has been suggested are deliberate tactics to provoke protest crowds to riot is not something I see much need to debate. The truly fascinating aspect of McIntyre's story is what it reveals about how the British understand disability: namely, that real disabled people are not whole human beings.

The attitude is that there are two types of disabled person: there are real disabled people, who are quiet and grateful and utterly incapable of any sort of personal agency whatsoever, and fake disabled people – people like Jody McIntyre, who are disqualified from being truly disabled by virtue of having personality, ambition, outside interests and, in this case, the *cojones* to stand up to a corrupt and duplicitous government.

This remarkable Catch-22 clause, whereby the authorities can claim that any disabled person who criticises them on disability or any other issues must, *ipso facto*, not actually be disabled, does not only affect how individuals like McIntyre are treated. It directly influences policymaking in the most clinical and ruthless of ways. Bear in mind that, besides its highly publicised cuts to secondary and higher education funding, this government is also taking away benefits from disabled people: housing benefit, income support, the mobility component of Disability Living Allowance and other vital sources of funding are being cut back to the bone or removed entirely.

The withdrawal of the mobility component for people in residential care is a particularly nasty slash, as this benefit allows people with mobility difficulties a modicum of independence, something that, in the eyes of this government, real disabled people should neither want nor need. It pays for taxis, motorised scooters and wheelchairs – wheelchairs like the one the police damaged when they tipped Jody McIntyre right out of it.

On top of this, those claiming sickness benefits or Employment and Support Allowance will be obliged to take another round of punishing tests that are acknowledged to be designed specifically to prevent hundreds of thousands of benefit recipients from receiving any more money.

'Currently, nearly a third of all disabled people live below the official poverty line, with a quarter of families with disabled children unable to afford heating,' said Eleanor, a spokesperson for Disabled People Against Cuts (DPAC) who protested in central London today about what the group sees as a direct assault on disability rights in the UK. 'A tenth of all disabled women have incomes under £31 per week,' she said. 'And yet, the government intends to slash the number of claimants on Disability Living Allowance by 20 per cent, although the fraud rate is estimated to be a mere 0.5 per cent.'

Six months ago, when I was helping my disabled partner, who has severe mobility issues and chronic pain, prepare to claim DLA, we realised that he would not be considered sufficiently disabled unless he was prepared actually to demonstrate to a partial outside observer that he could not walk 30 steps without falling on his face. It was humiliating and it was inhumane, and eventually, like many others, we gave up. The subsequent poverty and the stress of watching my partner struggle to cope with his disability with no support eventually ended the relationship and left me with a profound understanding of how successive administrations have used welfare reform to humiliate and terrorise the most vulnerable into abject complaisance.

All of this is justified by the assumption that most people claiming disability benefits are, to put it bluntly, faking it. That's right, hundreds of thousands of people with mental or physical health problems that prevent them from working have the audacity to want a scrap of agency, a life that is in any way full or useful, so they must be faking it all.

This government would prefer it if people with disabilities were not also people with opinions, desires and personalities. This government would prefer it if there were a clear demarcation line between people with the ability to stand up for themselves in any way whatsoever and people who are entirely reliant on the state, who ought to know their place: head bowed, hands outstretched, mouth shut, uncomplaining, accustomed to poverty and public derision. This government, with its utter contempt for the entire concept of social security, would prefer to be obliged to support only those who are prepared to sacrifice absolutely every bit of personal agency, to put up and shut up.

This is, of course, utter rubbish. This is not a Victorian melodrama, with the world neatly divided into people who are whole and hale and mawkish, abject cripples who are terminally grateful for any charity thrown to them and permanently followed around by a chorus of tiny violins. In the real world, the only difference between people with disabilities and everyone else is that people with disabilities sometimes need a little extra support to live the best lives that they can. They should get that support – and they should not have to ask nicely.

HEY, DAVE: OUR SOCIETY'S BIGGER THAN YOURS

18 February 2011

The words 'big society' will be written on the tombstone of this Conservative government. They were written on the side of the Treasury – which is, in effect, the same thing – in angry spray-can letters during the riots in December. The people of this country will not mutely acquiesce to the mortgaging of civic society to pay off the debts of the super-rich. A new social spirit is on the move, but it is not the one that the Tories envisage.

As vital public services are being dismantled, people are occupying their local libraries instead of volunteering to staff them. Instead of wealthy parents setting up academies, there are education activists running free schools for all-comers in empty mansions in Fitzrovia. David Cameron's big society branding platform imagined us 'taking responsibility for the people around us'. He didn't imagine that we'd be doing it by standing together on picket lines.

The Tory rhetoric around the big society is breathtakingly patronising. It's not just the awful name, which makes it sound suspiciously as though our politics were now a slick children's television show, fronted by puppets. It's not just the glib way in which the parties in government are slashing training programmes at a time when youth unemployment is nearing a million, while holding lavish fundraising balls where millionaire donors can bid for top City internships for their sons and daughters. And it's not just the way they declare that we can no longer afford to care for our sick and disabled, while they somehow find spare cash for tens of billions of pounds in tax breaks for banks. It's that they have the gall to do all of this and then to suggest that it is ordinary voters who have lost their sense of social responsibility.

Guess what? Enforced hardship makes people band together and now we have an uprising that's far bigger and more social than Cameron could have imagined. Who are the authors of this revolution? Check your mirror. It's true that there are career activists and romantic student adventurers leading the charge. But the real revolt taking place in Britain involves every one of us, whether we like it or not. It's about whether you and I are willing to let our society be broken apart and sold to unelected global financiers or whether we have the courage to stake our claim.

The sort of dissent that petrifies the powerful has an everyday face. It's the 12-year-old who organises a picket of the Prime Minister's constituency office to save his youth centre. It's the woman with progressive multiple sclerosis who builds an online resistance network to fight the cuts to disability benefits. It's the striking call-centre worker. It's the 16-year-old with no hope of affording university who misses class to protest in front of the Houses of Parliament and the teacher who lets her go.

'David Cameron, can't you see? We're the big society!' chanted members of the protest group UK Uncut at a recent demonstration against corporate tax avoidance. Cameron is about to meet the real big society and he's about to discover that it's more than a branding exercise. It's about real people standing together to fight real injustice. It's called socialism.

IN DEFENCE OF SQUATTING

20 February 2011

Squatting is such an ugly word. It implies that young, skint and precariously housed people who set up homes in the vacant properties of the landed elite are somehow crouching there to defecate, rather than building communities in dead investment space abandoned by the rich.

The education activists who were evicted last weekend from Guy Ritchie's £6 million Fitzrovia mansion have been portrayed by the tabloids as a 'gang' of criminal yobs. They are nothing of the kind: not least because they have done nothing illegal by creating a Free School, designed to 'cultivate equality through collaboration' in an empty mansion belonging to a millionaire film director who already owns several more.

Squatting empty buildings is not a criminal offence. It is, in fact, an ancient right, a tradition that can be traced back over centuries of popular dissent and pragmatism. After the Second World War, thousands of ex-servicemen and families with nowhere else to go began to squat in London, and their stoicism and ingenuity was vindicated by public opinion.

The social history of Britain – from the Kett rebellion to the True Levellers to Peterloo, from the Suffragettes to the environmental activists who have just prevented this government from selling the forests to timber companies – is largely the history of working people trying to stop the rich from hoarding space, assets and rights that were once held in common. It is a history of the struggle of ordinary people to build lives for themselves in a world whose physical boundaries are set by the interests of property and of profit, and the Really Free School, along with other similar groups that are being set up as I write, represent, in their own words, 'the latest chapter in a long history of resistance'.

Five centuries after Robert Kett and his brother were tortured and hanged for demanding that 'no lord of no manor shall common upon the commons', the struggle is ongoing. In a country where there is increasingly little space for the poor, the young and the needy, where benefit cuts and the decimation of the voluntary sector are likely to leave many more individuals and community groups with nowhere to live and work, the re-appropriation of space by occupation and squatting is set to become more important than ever.

It is not my place to speak for or on behalf of the Really Free School, which has moved to a new location following its eviction from Fitzroy Square. The space, with its classes on law and literature, its free kitchen and its library, speaks for itself. Despite the spiteful portrayal of these squatters in the tabloids, not all of their new neighbours wanted the Free Schoolers to leave.

'The Really Free School has taken a house that was not being used and created a space where ordinary people could get together and learn from each other and draw attention to the state of education in Britain,' wrote Linus Rees, chair of trustees of the Fitzrovia Neighbourhood Association, which represents the 'poor and marginalised' residents of the area as well as more privileged locals such as Ritchie.

'In Fitzrovia, hostels that support vulnerable people are due to be shut and community services are under threat because of the government cuts,' said Rees. 'These young people are a credit to their generation and we would do well to embrace their enthusiasm for trying to bring about a better society.'

Many squatted communities have been welcomed by local residents. Recently, a residential squat in Dalston was preserved after neighbours joined a campaign to support the occupiers. St Agnes Place, a street in Kennington that was squatted for over 30 years, provided social centres, hostels and street parties for the local community and was an international destination for artists and musicians until it was finally evicted in 2005 and the buildings demolished.

Squatting is not a criminal offence, but a moral question, and the question is simple. Do you think that, in a country where half a million people are homeless and a further half million 'hidden homeless' are sleeping on their friends' sofas because they have nowhere else to go, in a country where the housing crisis is so acute that people are being sent to prison for begging, it is sensible for half a million residential properties to be standing empty, accruing capital for the well-off?

Do you believe that, in a country where 650,000 households are overcrowded, where the government has declared that it can no longer afford to help the landless sick, disabled and poorly paid to sleep safely because it needs to give tax breaks to bankers, it is right that so many commercial buildings are vacant, boarded up and patrolled by private security firms? Do you consider it fair that there is less than no room for the young, the poor, the disabled and the disenfranchised in this society, while the rich control more space than they know what to do with?

It is manifestly in the interests of those who own and hold all this disused property, including the millionaires who make up the Cabinet, to misrepresent Britain's 15,000 squatters and occupiers as – in the words of *The Times* – a 'dangerous scourge'. Otherwise the hundreds of thousands of people paying 90 per cent of their salary for pokey rooms hours from their places of work might start getting ideas. The community organisers might start getting ideas. The charities, the homeless families and the youth groups struggling to survive might start thinking, 'Hey – there's a lot of empty space going spare. Why don't we just take the space for ourselves?'

There is so much that could be done with Britain's empty properties. The women's refuges and asylum centres whose funding is about to be withdrawn could use the space to continue the valuable work they do in local communities, work that is about to be abruptly curtailed by Conservative funding cuts. More free schools and community centres are already being planned across and outside London. But the reoccupation of private space is more than just pragmatism in the face of austerity.

Occupation is a deeply political act, whether it is done for years or, as with this week's UK Uncut protests, which re-appropriated bank branches and turned them into reading groups and children's centres, for mere minutes. There are reasons that so many banners hanging outside occupied public spaces and the placards on public marches read 'resist; strike; occupy'. Occupations are just as important as marches and strikes in the context of resistance movements. They allow us to redraw the physical contours of our political reality. They provide people with centres to share skills and build links in spaces that are truly common, spaces that we do not have to enter under sufferance. They respond to a government seeking to turn every public asset into a private revenue stream, by turning private assets into public resources. And they make it clear that private property need not be the whole of the law.

Less than 100 years ago, women (and most men who did not own property) were not permitted to vote; we were not considered real citizens. Today, a barely-elected government underwrites the interests of a landed elite while cutting benefits and services for those who already live on next to nothing, because it does not consider those without property to be its constituency, because those without property do not win elections for the parliamentary class.

I believe that in these circumstances squatting, occupation and the re-appropriation of disused private property is more than merely appropriate: it is a deeply moral and courageous response, a response that neighbours, councils and local representatives should fully support.

INSIDE THE GADDAFI HOUSE[28]

15 March 2011

'My family had to leave Libya just to survive,' says a young bearded man in spectacles, perching awkwardly on a white leather sofa. We are in the front room of Saif al-Islam al-Gaddafi's mansion in Hampstead Garden Suburb, recently expropriated by activists working in alliance with Libyan exiles. An hour earlier, I had passed through an open window near some ugly imported ferns belonging to Muammar al-Gaddafi's son, having been invited to meet the members of the new Free Libyan Embassy.

We drink stewed tea from Saif's best china and eat cheese sandwiches using his silver cutlery, while the young man, Abdulla, tells me about how his uncle was 'disappeared' by Saif's father. 'In Libya, people disappear all the time. There was a prison massacre where 1,200 people died. They poured cement over the bodies.' Abdulla nervously adjusts his glasses. 'It's important that people know we're not creating a civil war for no reason.'

Nearly every room in this enormous house boasts a large, flat-screen television. The occupiers have set each one to al-Jazeera, for rolling coverage of the people's revolutions that are sweeping the Arab world. Televised gunfire echoes in the marble hallway as Jay, 25, explains how activists from the London squatter movement took over the Gaddafi mansion,

---

28. The Libyans involved in this article wanted their names to be known; other names have been changed.

moving in secretly and putting up notices declaring their intention to hold the empty house under English common law. 'We wanted to show our solidarity the best way we know how,' he says.

'It's a symbolic and practical reclamation of private property that belongs to the Libyan people. It's about their struggle, which is why the place has been handed over to the Libyans as a place to organise and a safe space for refugees,' Jay says. 'People have been arriving in support from all over the UK.' The tabloids have portrayed the occupiers as drunken anarchists but this is, in Jay's words, 'total bollocks'. 'On the first night, people came down thinking there would be a squat party and we turned them away. They didn't seem to realise how seriously we're taking this,' he explains.

'At first, we were elated that we'd managed to pull it off. Then the Libyans turned up and they were elated. But once they started to get reports about family and friends being killed, the atmosphere changed. We were watching Zawiyah burning on al-Jazeera and someone saw his own house. It was terrible.'

Jay takes me on a tour over four floors of hushed opulence, each several times the size of an ordinary London flat. 'It's worth nearly £11 million,' he says. Under the kitchen is a cosy entertainment complex, complete with pool, Jacuzzi, sauna and a private cinema done out in suede, the pews so thick and warm you could sleep on them – which people have been doing. On the corner of one aisle a bare duvet lies, neatly folded. Everything here is white, bright and glistening: white leather sofas, marble floors, silver candlesticks adorning pristine white walls. The only note of colour is in one of the guest bedrooms, where a Libyan flag has been draped over the TV.

Fearing the spectacle of bailiffs dragging Libyans out of the private property of a Gaddafi, at a time when the UK government is desperately downplaying its erstwhile support for the dictator, the authorities have kept their distance. But that doesn't mean that there have been no attempts to get the occupiers to leave.

'Last night, at about four in the morning, someone came to the door,' Jay says. According to Abdulla, 'It was a well-dressed Arab person, [wearing] nice clothes and gold. When I asked him what he was doing here so late, he said, "I want to make you an offer." He told us: "I have £40,000 in cash. You can have it if you leave immediately." No amount of money could make us leave this house. It's not a financial issue.'

On the sofa opposite, a quiet man called Ambarak suddenly speaks up in Arabic. 'What's a life worth?' he says, as Abdulla translates softly. 'What are 100,000 lives worth?' Ambarak perches on the edge of the sofa, looking out of place in his *keffiyeh* and scuffed trainers.

'I'm talking about people being shot by snipers in the street. I'm talking about family members selling dry bread to live. They ask what the west should do, but they've known about [Muammar] Gaddafi for years,' he continues in broken English. 'They did nothing. The petrol … ' – he rubs his fingers together in a 'money' gesture, grinning without humour. 'My brother has disappeared in the fighting. We haven't heard from him, we have no way of contacting him.' Ambarak goes very quiet. 'Excuse me, please. I must go and pray.'

'The resources that come out of Libya should belong to the people but that petrol money goes somewhere else,' says Abdulla. 'All those close to Gaddafi have places like this to live. There are some who are heartless and will do anything for a comfortable life.' Ambarak's family is in Misurata, where fierce fighting continues. 'They say on the phone that they can hear shooting and tanks are coming down the street. My cousin has died, [as have] my friend, my neighbours.'

An influx of neighbours bearing food terminates the interview. A young man wearing a Libyan flag like a cape takes the cups politely to the sink. He is a long way from home. 'We all want to go home,' says Abdulla. 'But not to Libya as it is now.'

Details of Original Publication

The following chapters first appeared in the *New Statesman*: 'Inside the Millbank Tower riots', 'Inside the Whitehall Kettle', 'Protesting the Turner Prize', 'Inside the Parliament Square Kettle', 'A Right Royal Poke', 'No Sex, No Drugs and No Leaders', 'What Really Happened in Trafalgar Square', 'The Gulag of Desire', 'In Defence of Cunt', 'What *Sun* Readers Swallow with their Corn Flakes', 'The Sexy Way to Die', 'Vajazzled and Bemused', 'Galliano's Fashionable Beliefs', 'The Princess Craze is no Fairy Tale', 'Skinny Porn', 'Violence Against Women in Tahrir Square', 'Zionism, Chauvinism and the Nature of Rape', 'A Modesty Slip for Misogyny', 'Charlie Sheen's Problem with Women', 'The Shame is All Theirs', 'Undercover With the Young Conservatives', 'Buns, Bunting and Retro-Imperialism', 'This is England', 'Poppy Day is the Opium of the People', 'Michael Gove and the Imperialists', 'The Power of the Intern', 'Strictly come Scrounging?', 'Poverty Pimps: Selling out the Disabled', 'A Tale of Three Parties', 'The Social Mobility Scam', 'Facebook, Capitalism and Geek Entitlement', 'Girls, Tattoos and Men who Hate Women', 'Julie Burchill's Imperialist Rant over Israel', 'Baby Boomers', 'It's all over for Sex-and-Shopping Feminism', 'Insurrection on Oxford Street', 'This Is No Conspiracy', 'The Revolution Will Be Civilised', 'How the Disabled were Dehumanised', 'Hey, Dave: Our Society's Bigger than Yours' and 'In Defence of Squatting'.

'Talking About a Revolution' and 'Burlesque Laid Bare' first appeared in the *Guardian*.

'Pickling Dissent' first appeared in the *Independent*.

The interview with China Miéville first appeared in the *Morning Star*.

'Me, the Patriarchy and my Big Red Pen', 'Bah, Humbug', 'Is that a Truncheon in Your Pocket?' and 'One Man and his Tent' first appeared in *Penny Red*.

'Beyond Noughtie Girls' first appeared in *The F-Word*.

'Lies in London' first appeared in *Boing Boing*.

'I Shall Wear Midnight' first appeared in *Io9*.